OUR FATHER, OUR MOTHER

MARY AND THE FACES OF GOD
BIBLICAL AND PASTORAL REFLECTIONS

George T. Montague, S.M.

Published by:
  Franciscan University Press
  Franciscan University of Steubenville
  Steubenville, OH 43952

Printed in the United States of America

ISBN: O-940535-28-9

CONTENTS

PREFACE

Just north of St. Louis, where I wrote this book, three great rivers become one: the Missouri, the Illinois and the Mississippi. Each river has modest beginnings, grows as it is fed by a vast watershed, then offers its life to a community of rivers to make the nation's largest waterway.

This book is the confluence of three rivers in my life. The name of the first river is "Father." It is fed by the experience of my own father, of others who have "fathered" me in life-giving ways, of my own "fathering" of others. Glorious moments, painful moments. Great achievements. And mistakes. It is also the story of my discovery of God the Father. When I was 41 years old, an ordained priest for twelve years, I was graced with a spiritual experience of God as Father. It was a real break-through, a new departure in my pilgrimage. As a result, my favorite theme for conferences, workshops and retreats, in this country as well as in the other continents to which I was called, especially during my six years in Asia, became the Lord's prayer. This experience and ministry was abetted, of course, by my scriptural studies and especially by my study and teaching of the Gospel of Matthew, in which the fatherhood of God plays a key role. It was a matter of amazement to me how the theme of God's fatherhood opened retreatants to a spiritual liberation as they discovered to what extent they were God's children. It became obvious to me that *my* river, like the Lord's prayer itself, was *our* river. The river "Father" flowed not only through my life but through the life and the history of the universal church.

But there was an equally strong river called "Mother," likewise formed from childhood experiences of my own mother and swelled by adult experiences of nurturance. It too found a transcendental expression in Mary. I was led to join a religious community bearing the name of Mary, with a founder who had a rich spirituality derived from Mary's spiritual motherhood. Today this river is also flowing strongly in the church, for we are seeing a Marian renewal that rivals that of the fifties. As of this writing, it is estimated that more than eleven million pilgrims have visited Medjugorje. Whatever the final judgment of the church on the phenomena there, it is obvious that Marian devotion and practice is on the rise. At the same time, with my biblical background, I have been uncomfortable with some aspects of Marian devotion which I have witnessed. Particularly I am concerned that some Marian devotion, even when it leads to Christ, hardly ever gives a glance at God the Father. If Marian devotion is authentic, it should lead to the Trinity. It is destined to become part of a greater river.

The third river that has fed this book is the contemporary concern about language, particularly in the church of North America: "sexist" and "exclusive" vs. "non-sexist" and "inclusive." "Glory be to the Single Parent, the Only Child, and the Holy Spirit"—this inclusive doxology proposed, tongue-in-cheek, by one of my biblical colleagues, illustrates the quagmire we have gotten into in the last decade in English discourse in general and the fact that even the skirts of that "queen of the sciences," which in more "sexist" language days we called theology, have been caught in the maelstrom. Can we talk about God as Father any more? Should "he" be neutered? Should we revise the Lord's prayer to begin,

"Our Father and Mother?" And if there is a motherhood in God, how does the tradition of Mary as mother relate to God as mother?

Perhaps it would be more modest not to attempt to address all these issues in a single volume. But it seems to me that only in deeply understanding the first two rivers which flow through the tradition of the church can we successfully address the meeting of the third. Some of those concerned with God language have dismissed the Marian dimension as irrelevant, while others have held that Mary really functions as a goddess. Some see the title "Father" as reinforcing a patriarchal system. Some see the image of Mary as a cop-out: she is a wimpish woman who surrenders to male tyranny and therefore cannot be a model for the modern woman. Others, however, argue that she is, in her Magnificat especially, the leader of all liberation.

This book does not pretend to answer all the questions raised, especially in the matter of language. It is, however, a modest attempt to build a bridge of understanding between disparate circles of concern in the church today—circles that many Christians find inside themselves as well. By going to our biblical roots, and exploring first the image and the language of "Father," I hope then to show how Mary *functions* in the work of the Trinitarian life within us. It is not so much the doctrines about Mary that interest me here, as the way she is used by the Holy Spirit in the formation and growth of Christians.

In the first part I explore the masculine and feminine faces of God as revealed in the Bible. Other religions have other ways of dealing with the masculine and feminine. The Greek and Roman myths multiplied male and female divinities, and so it is still in Hinduism today. When looking at a statue of the Buddha, it is impossible to tell, in most cases, whether the image is male or female. In the Buddhist shrine of Asuka, Japan, the larger-than-life statue, if viewed from one side, reveals a male face; if viewed from the other, a female face. Israel's monotheism was much more discreet in dealing with this issue, but both masculine and feminine imagery emerge. For if God has created humankind "in his own image, male and female he created them" (Gen 1:26), then, although the *distinction* of the sexes is found in the creature, the *origin* of that distinction is in the creator. And therefore all its richness as well. But that richness is mediated in biblical revelation in a unique way, which the first two chapters explore.

In the mainstream of the Christian tradition, the feminine aspect of God has been experienced through Mary, the mother of the Lord. Part Two, after listening to a typical contemporary experience of Mary, seeks an understanding of the Marian experience in the biblical theology of the Holy Spirit. Three biblical motifs (a word I prefer to use for "themes") appear central to this understanding of Mary as instrument of the Spirit in the foundational phase of our faith and in the ongoing formation of Christians—the Queen Mother, Virgin Daughter Zion, and Mother Zion. The final chapter offers a modest conclusion concerning the Father-Mother question. Two appendices offer some additional contemporary witnesses to the action of Mary in the lives of Christians.

I cannot pretend to be the first to explore some of the aspects I have treated here. The poet Paul Claudel, sociologist Andrew Greeley, and theologians Leonardo Boff and Manfred Hauke, to mention only four of different nations and specializations, have already broken ground here. And the feminist debate has already produced an abundance of literature on language and theology. Though I did my research independently, I appreciate the work of these predecessors even when I have fundamental disagreements with some of them. In writing *Our Father, Our Mother,* I have tried to combine scholarship, pastoral concern, the growth of the Christian life and experience in a way that hopefully will speak to the non-specialist as well as to the theologian. My hope is that this book will not only be a bridge of understanding but also an inspiration for spiritual growth in a Christian life that can be all the more Trinitarian for its being Marian.

George T. Montague, S.M.
Feast of Mary, Mother of God, 1990

PART ONE

GOD AS FATHER AND MOTHER

Chapter One

ABBA: THE SPECIFIC REVELATION OF JESUS

Jesus grew up in a culture shaped by the Bible. In the synagogue every Sabbath he heard readings from the law and the prophets; he probably knew the Psalms by heart. He daily recited the Shema: "Hear, O Israel: The Lord our God is one Lord; and you shall love the Lord your God will all your heart, and with all your soul, and with all your might" (Deut 6:4-5).

In the midst of all of this he learned the traditional names of God: *El, Elohim* (God), *Adonai* (Lord—the spoken term for the never-uttered written name *Yahweh*), plus the various poetic images, King, Rock, Fortress, Shepherd, to mention only a few. Given what we know of Jesus and his teaching, however, the title that must have struck him most was *Father*. It appears hardly more than a dozen times as a name for God in the Old

Testament[1], and always as the formal Hebrew *Abh*. God is the Father of orphans (Ps 68:6), of the people Israel (Deut 32:6; Jer 3:4; 31:9; Mal 1:6; Is 63:16; 64:7) or of the king who rules in God's name (2 Sam 7:14; Ps 89:27; 1 Chron 17:13; 22:10; 28:6).

What the Scriptural "Father" Meant to Jesus

What did the title mean in the Jewish heritage that came down to Jesus? Was it the canonization of patriarchal oppression, as some contemporary feminists claim?[2] The evidence points in another direction. Many of the surrounding peoples used the image of father for their divine progenitor, a god from whom they were descended. This led them not only to idealize their nation but also to proscribe jealously any departure from land or family. "Their salvation depends on their staying at home."[3] But Israel as a people began with a simple human being Abraham, whom the Lord commanded to leave his land and his father's house (Gen 12:1), setting a pattern for subsequent ruptures of the natural order by God's grace, either to save or to create anew. Thus even Abraham's attempt to assure his heritage naturally through Hagar and Ishmael is rejected in favor of the promised child of grace to be born of Sarah, Isaac, who is saved from human sacrifice by divine intervention. The tribes in Egypt are saved by a mighty act of God's grace. And so on. At the heart of this pattern is the notion of election and covenant. And it is precisely within that theology that the Israelite image of God as Father becomes comprehensible. It is not a fatherhood of generation, but a fatherhood of *adoption:*

> So you shall say to Pharaoh: Thus says the LORD: Israel is my son, my firstborn. Hence I tell you: Let

14

my son go, that he may serve me (Ex 4:22-23).

When Israel was a child I loved him, out of Egypt I called my son (Hos 11:1).

...you saw [in Egypt and in the desert] how the LORD, your God, carried you, as a man carries his child, all along your journey until you arrived at this place (Deut 1:31). Is he not your father who created you? Has he not made you and established you? (Deut 32:6)

Have we not all the one Father?
    Has not the one God created us?
Why then do we break faith with each other,
    violating the covenant of our fathers (Mal 2:10)?

These texts all refer to the Lord's deliverance of Israel from Egypt and the covenant by which he "created" them as a people, liberating them from their oppressors and promising them a future. "Father" fits this convenant symbolism because God's intervention was an act of adoption, powerfully conveying to what extent these people became *his*. As with the covenant itself, the image of father thus means first of all grace and belonging, and only subsequently obedience[4].

It is precisely to evoke God's loving kindness that the prophets use "Father" to call Israel to repentance.

I had thought:
    How I should like to treat you as sons,
And give you a pleasant land,
    a heritage most beautiful among the nations!
You would call me, "My Father," I thought,
    and never cease following me...
Return, rebellious children
    and I will cure you of your rebelling (Jer 3:19-22).

And the response of the repentant poet echoes the pity and mercy the nation expects to find from its father-God:

> Look down from heaven and regard us
>> from your holy and glorious palace!
> Where is your zealous care and your might,
>> your surge of pity and your mercy?
> O Lord, hold not back,
>> for you are our *father.*
> Were Abraham not to know us,
>> nor Israel to acknowledge us,
> You, LORD, are our *father,*
>> our redeemer you are named forever (Is 63:15-16).

This text also shows that Israel's concept of its God's fatherhood was not a univocal transfer of human fatherhood to the divinity. God's fatherhood is something utterly reliable, beyond the limitations of the best and primal Israelite father, Abraham. (A distant preparation for "Our Father, who art in heaven.")

The final father image in the book of Isaiah is soaked with loving surrender and trust:

> . . . you have hidden your face from us
>> and have delivered us up to our guilt.
> Yet, O LORD, you are our *father;*
>> we are the clay and you the potter:
>> we are all the work of your hands (Is 64:6-7).

Maternal Imagery

That this was not a male versus female image appears from the ease with which the prophets flowed from the father image into the maternal aspects of God's love. In Hos 11:1-4, for example, it is not possible to distinguish whether the Lord is describing himself as father or mother to Israel, the beloved child:

> When Israel was a child I loved him,
> out of Egypt I called my son...
> Yet it was I who taught Ephraim to walk,
> who took them in my arms;...
> I fostered them like one
> who raises an infant to his cheeks;
> Yet, though I stooped to feed my child,
> they did not know that I was their healer.

These were activities more normally performed by the mother in ancient Israel.[5] We might also note that the Hebrew word for compassion, *rahamim*, used in the Old Testament so frequently for God, is simply the plural of the word for "womb."

In Numbers 11, a passage heavily influenced by the prophetic movement, Moses complains:

> "Why do you treat your servant so badly?...Why are you so displeased with me that you burden me with all this people? Was it I who conceived all this people? or was it I who gave them birth, that you tell me to carry them at my bosom, like a foster father carrying an infant, to the land you have promised under oath to their fathers?" (Num 11:11-12)

The implication is obviously that God is both mother and father to Israel, since Moses objects to having this dual role "dumped" on him. Deuteronomy 32:18 also paints this exodus-covenant "begetting of Israel" in the imagery of both parents:

> You were unmindful of the Rock that begot you [father], you forgot the God who gave you birth [mother].

By combining father and mother images of God, the prophets were able to hold within a strict monotheism popular piety, which was open to the constant seduction of Canaanite male and female divinities, a cult mocked by Jeremiah:

> They who say to a piece of wood, "You are my father," and to a stone, "You gave me birth" (Jer 2:27).

In prophetic thought, therefore, the image of father was not primarily one of authority and power, but one of adoptive love, covenant bonding, tenderness, and compassion. It combined what we understand today as the roles of both father and mother.[6]

Address and Metaphor

Still, we must do justice to the fact that the title "Mother" is never used in direct address to God; rather female metaphors are used to enrich and extend the basic metaphor "Father."[7] There is no evidence, then, that the biblical authors thought "Mother" and "Father" were simply interchangeable realities. There are historical and theological reasons for this reticence which we shall see in the next chapter. For the moment, however, it would not be out of place to suggest that the two titles correspond to important complementary functions of parenthood deeply imbedded in the human person from infancy. John W. Miller summarizes the findings of the social sciences when he writes:

> . . . for an adequate understanding of the significance of the father-role some awareness is needed, first of all, of the strength of the bond that typically exists between *mothers* and children by

virtue of their symbiotic tie during pregnancy, birth and nursing. It is this biologically determined relationship, so essential in laying the foundations of healthy development, that shapes those qualities usually associated with mothering: unconditional availability, receptivity, and tenderness. Fathers, on the other hand, when effectively present to their families, insert themselves into the bond between mother and child as a "second other" by an initiative very much like that of adoption. Where this initiative is energetic and winsome, developmental psychology teaches us, an essential autonomy from the mother is fostered, and children of both sexes are significantly helped in orienting themselves to the cultural universe outside the home with its laws and ethical norms. Maternal values are not thereby repudiated — fathers too may embody tender, mother-like attributes without ceasing to be fathers — but the exclusivity of the mother bond is challenged by an authority that separates the child and orients it towards its personal future in extrafamilial society.[8]

There is then, an important revealed content to the metaphor *Father* when applied to God, a content corresponding to a deep psychological function. At that level, it has nothing to do with the oppression of women, nor, as we shall now see in greater detail, with the exclusion of intimacy.

Jesus' Name for God

Of all the Old Testament titles for God, none not even the formal *Abh,* "Father," satisfied Jesus. In the gradual maturing of his human consciousness, which is evident from the New Testament (Luke 2:52: "Jesus advanced [in] wisdom and age and favor before God and man"), his understanding of God developed out of human experiences, and those were not directly religious ones. It was not in the synagogue that Jesus' most determining experience of fatherhood occurred. It was in his home at Nazareth.

The Jewish Talmud tells us that when a child begins to speak, the first words he or she learns are *abba* and *imma*. These terms may not mean exactly what our titles "daddy" and "mama" mean, but they come close, for there is no doubt that the terms are the informal, familiar titles of intimacy.[9] For Jesus, then, the first person whom he addressed as *abba* was not God but Joseph.[10] As his human consciousness developed and came into its own — that is, as he began to reach beyond the names he had learned for God and sought a name that would express his personal experience and understanding of God — he chose the familiar, intimate name he had given Joseph as a child: *abba*. This title stuck with Jesus his entire adult life, for nothing else explains why Mark, writing in Greek, would suddenly revert to the Aramaic original in describing Jesus' prayer in Gethsemane: "Abba, Father, all things are possible to you. . ." (Mk 14:36). Though elsewhere the evangelists do not bother to reproduce the Aramaic, it is likely that behind most, if not all, of the Greek usages of "father" was Jesus' Aramaic, *Abba*.[11] Though Jesus used many other metaphors in his teaching *about* God, in all his prayers Jesus never *addresses* God by any other title than *Father*.[12] This is significant considering that Jewish prayers used predominantly other, more sovereign titles for God, and in late Judaism the relationship with God as Father becomes less a privilege conferred on Israel as a people and increasingly dependent on the merit of the few.[13] Today even those scholars most skeptical about being able to recover the words of the historical Jesus are willing to concede that the word *Abba* for God comes from Jesus himself. And they do so because that word stands in contrast to all previous names by which God was addressed in the Old Testament and in the prayer literature of late Judaism, even the formal name "Father."[14]

When asked by his disciples for a prayer formula, Jesus gave them this name for God. Though our Greek texts of Matthew 6:9 and Luke 11:2 do not have the Aramaic *Abba* in their texts of the Lord's prayer, Paul's repeated use of it in the context of community prayer (Gal 4:6; Rom 8:15) indicates it was commonly known and used. Thus we can be morally certain that Jesus not only used *Abba* for his personal prayer but taught it to his disciples as well.

If that is so, then we are the very heart of the revelation of Jesus, and that title cannot be discarded without dismantling what is unique about Jesus' revelation. "No one knows the Son except the Father, and no one knows the Father except the Son and anyone to whom the Son wishes to reveal him" (Mt 11:27). "No one has ever seen God. The only-begotten, who is God, ever at the Father's side, has revealed him" (John 1:18). If the Lord's prayer is the essence of the gospel, it is because all that Jesus came to reveal flows from the revelation of the Father's name: "I revealed your *name* to those whom you gave me. . ." (John 17:6).

Implications

And what, for Jesus, was implied in *Abba*? As foundation, he took over all that was implied in the Old Testament use of the formal word *Abh,* which, as we saw above, meant election, the bond of covenant love, mercy and compassion. But most of all *Abba* was a word of *intimacy*—Jesus' intimacy with the Father and the incredible degree of intimacy God wishes to establish with each human being and with the whole human family. There is, of course, a qualitative difference between Jesus' relationship with the Father and that of the disciples, as appears from the fact that Jesus speaks of "my Father" and "your Father" but never uses "Our Father" in his teaching other than in Matthew 6:9, where he tells his *disciples* to say "Our Father." Nevertheless, it is in and with Jesus that the disciples are caught up into the Father's intimate love.

But there is another implication of no less importance, and that involves the kind of life the disciples are to live. In Matthew, this can be seen most clearly in the Sermon on the Mount.[15] It is significant for our study here to note that the Sermon on the Mount is not addressed to the crowds in general but to the disciples in the sight of the crowds. The significance of this for the references in the Sermon to "your Father in heaven" should not be lost. At the level of Matthew's redaction, if not actually in the original teaching of Jesus, the implication appears to be that in order to experience truly the fatherhood of God, one must become a disciple of Jesus.

But from this experience other behavioral consequences follow. Because the disciples are children of this Father, they are to be perfect as he is perfect, they must love as he loves, and that means loving even one's enemies (Mt 5:43-48). Alms are to be given secretly so that the Father alone may see them (6:4); prayer is to be made in the privacy of the heart, for such is the prayer the Father hears (6:6). No need to multiply prayers, because the Father knows our needs even before we ask (6:8; 7:11). Fasting is to be done for the Father, not for a human audience (6:18). Trust in the Father means not to be worried about life, food, clothes, or tomorrow (6:23-34). Above all, because the Father forgives, the disciple must forgive (6:12, 14-15). The forgiveness the Father gives can be lost if the disciple is not willing to share that forgiveness with others (18:21-35). Because God is Father, all those in the community are brothers and sisters, making the breakdown of relationships a most severe, even a blasphemous thing (5:21-26). The command to honor father and mother is reinforced (Mt 19:19), but conformity to patriarchal traditions and attachments must yield to the claims of the fatherhood of God (Mt 8:21-22; 12:50). Jesus even says, "Call no one on earth your father, for you have one father who is in heaven" (Mt 23:9). Finally, as a climax to the gospel, Jesus reveals himself as brother not just to the community but to everyone in need. To those who have shown kindness to him in that guise, Jesus opens the Father's kingdom (25:31-46).

It was his claim to such intimacy with God that eventually led to his being condemned to death for blasphemy (Mk 14:61-64). But in fact, it was the social consequences Jesus drew from his Abba consciousness that turned the powerful religious elite against him. Jesus created a barrier free, caste free community, dined with tax collectors and sinners, spoke to women in public, allowed them to touch him, counted them among his journeying companions, and chose them as the first witnesses of his resurrection. That was simply the horizontal dimension of his conviction that God is *Abba,* dearest father, who wants all to belong to his family as brothers and sisters. *Abba* was a word of liberation and communion.

The Father is Gift

But Jesus also insists that *Abba*, God cannot be learned from books or by merely mouthing the word. To know the Father is a gift, that is, an experience of grace:

> I give praise to you, Father, Lord of heaven and earth, for although you have hidden these things from the wise and the learned you have revealed them to the childlike. Yes, Father, such has been your gracious will. All things have been handed over to me by my Father. No one knows the Son, except the Father, and no one knows the Father except the Son and anyone to whom the Son wishes to reveal him (Mt 11:25-27).

That revelation is not merely an outward word. Many who heard Jesus' teaching about the Father refused to accept it. Paul makes it clear that it is the Holy Spirit alone who can enable the believer to cry, "Abba, Father" (Gal 4:6; Rom 8:15). And Luke implies the same by the fact that his catechism of prayer, opening with Jesus' teaching his disciples the words of the Lord's prayer, ends with his reminder that the Holy Spirit will be given by the Father to those who ask him (Luke 11:1-13).

Clearly, then, *Abba* is an inner word, an experience of faith given by the Holy Spirit. It is the exhilarating discovery of which the Muslim convert Begum Bilquis Sheik speaks in her book, *I Dared to Call Him Father*.[16] It changes one's entire view of the world. Since it is revealed only "to children" (Mt 11:25), it entails a conversion not merely from a life of sin but even from the self-made "good" life in order to receive the kingdom as a gift ("Whoever does not accept the kingdom of God like a child will not enter it" Mk 10:15). For only the child in heart can say, "Abba!"

Discovering the Father

It is possible for Christians to live their whole lives without really discovering the Father. I mean really discovering the Father—not just saying the "Our Father," or using the name of the Father in the Sign of the Cross, or any other Trinitarian formula. In my own life, the Father remained on the periphery of my spiritual consciousness until I was forty-one years old. I prayed to Jesus, I prayed to and through Mary, but I only came to experience deeply the Father after my involvement in the charismatic renewal, and specifically when some friends prayed over me on Christmas Eve, 1970. Many wonderful things happened as a result of that event; but most significant for me was the discovery of the Father.[17]

That discovery was only the beginning of a journey, for it involved facing squarely my experience of my earthly father and being healed of many memories. My father was a huge man. He was six feet tall, and his Texas boots below and his Stetson hat above made him a good three inches taller. He weighed 280 pounds and wore a size 55 belt. That alone would have been enough to make me fear him. I had a "cognitive" sense that he loved me, but not an "affective" sense. He used to take me hunting, fishing, and traveling with him on business. But he was a strong and autocratic disciplinarian, and several times I learned his 55-inch belt had another function besides holding up his pants. He also had a temper. And there were times when I felt his treatment of me was tyranny. (I detailed this in my book *Riding the Wind*.) Later I came to realize how this affective image of my earthly father was blocking my freedom to experience intimacy with Abba-God, and that it was really unfair to God and to myself to transfer to God my negative feelings about my father. Gradually I was led through a healing of memories, and though my father went to the Lord before I could complete the process face to face, I am now deeply grateful to the Lord for the father I had. I have come to realize how much I needed some of the things he was trying to give me, especially in strengthening my character to face the tough challenges of life. Sometimes he didn't know how to give; sometimes I didn't know how to receive. That healing, painful and progressive, liberated me even more to experience the powerful love of God the Father.

From that experience and those of countless others I have ministered to over the years, I have become convinced that most people's problems are not with God the Father, but with their own father or with other father figures in their lives. Thus I discovered that many persons' difficulty in calling God "Father," signaled, as in my own case, something that needed to surface to be confronted, healed and integrated in their own personal history—a growth challenge that would have been avoided had they chosen to eliminate "Father" from their religious vocabulary. In retreat after retreat I have helped hundreds of Christians claim their birthright: through the gift of the Holy Spirit and a healing of their relationship with their earthly father, to come to know Abba-God in a joyful, liberating, empowering way.

I also discovered that those who had a wholesome, loving relationship with their earthly father found the transfer to God as Father easy to make. One such retreatant, a woman happily married, stands out in my mind because of a recent letter in which she told me of the death of her father and what a beautiful experience she had with him in his last hours. I wrote back to her that, with such a father, it must have been easy to think of God as Father. To this she replied:

> Yes, Dad meant ever so much to me, and you are right in surmising that by knowing such a father, it was easy to think of God as a loving Father. At my Dad's knee I first learned about the love, mercy, compassion and faithfulness of God our Father and Jesus his Son . . . and as I came to the age of reason and understanding, it was Dad who first spoke to me of the wisdom and comfort of the Holy Spirit. He urged me when I was a young girl in school to pray to the Holy Spirit for wisdom, understanding and grace. So, long before I came into the Charismatic Renewal I was conscious of the Holy Spirit as a Person I could turn to, to lead and guide me through life. The charismatic experience of the outpouring of the Holy Spirit, especially as I received it in Patna at that memorable retreat, was an entering into and fulfillment of a familiar and recognized condition, as if I "had already been there" and was able to relive it with a new joy. I can never forget the surge of divine and Trinitarian love I experienced in my whole being as I could say "ABBA" with all the love of my life. Somewhere in the background of that experience my beloved Dad loomed. Through his love and kindness I experienced the potentiality of the infinite love of the Father — always calling, beckoning. Even now as he has passed into that infinity, I feel his presence inviting us to adoration and joy before the Eternal Father and the Beloved

of God, Jesus His Son. It's as if the dialogue is still going on, never to end, until we are all home again to share in that everlasting love.

There is another factor that has brought me to humble gratitude for the earthly father I had—and for what, without my realizing it, he was teaching me *positively* about God the Father. It was the realization of how blessed I was to have known and lived with my father at all! On returning to the States after six years in Nepal and India, where family stability has a much better track record than in the United States, I was shocked to witness how the breakup of the American family had accelerated in that short time. In 1970 there were 7,470,000 children under age eighteen living in a household with no father present, that is, about one child out of ten. By 1987 that number had almost doubled: 13,404,000 or 21.3 percent. That means that today more than one out of five children in America under eighteen have no father at home.[18]

When six students committed suicide in a Texas town, Americans were shocked. One of the boys was a handsome member of his high school football team. In a television interview his mother explained that her son had been depressed. When she asked him why, he answered: "Mom, you don't understand. You don't know what it is like to not have a father."[19] Dr. James Herzog, a psychiatrist at Children's Hospital Medical Center in Boston, in a study of seventy-two young children from single-parent homes, concluded that the absence of an active father figure was harmful, and most harmful to male toddlers eighteen to twenty-four months old. These children had recurring nightmares about monsters, which Herzog interpreted as a sign of displaced aggression and vulnerability.[20]

This alarming situation of the absent father in American society makes it problematical whether many in our country will ever be able to understand God as father. I, for one, believe that such an experience is possible, for two reasons. First, even for those deprived of the experience of their natural father, or whose experience of their actual father was negative, there are in most cases other father figures available from whom it is possible to learn what fathering means. I certainly have had many such father figures in my life. Second, coupled with that natural base, it is important to remember that learning to call and experience God as "Abba" is a work of grace, a gift of the Holy Spirit (Gal 4:6; Rom 8:15).

We have seen, then, that "Father" in Scripture is *integral* to the revelation of Jesus and consequently *irreplaceable* as his and the church's address to God. We have also seen its positive function in psychosocial and spiritual transformation. But is it *sufficient*? To this question we now turn.

NOTES

1. The number 14 is given by J. Jeremias in *The Lord's Prayer,* tr. J. Reumann (Philadelphia: Fortress Press, 1964), 18. The number 11 is given by R. Hamerton-Kelly, *God the Father: Theology and Patriarchy in the Teaching of Jesus* (Philadelphia: Fortress Press, 1979) 20, which is surely wrong, as it overlooks Ps 68:6. Since Protestant authors exclude Sirach and Wisdom from the Canon, they do not count the address of God as Father in Sir 23:1, 4; 51:10 (though the translation of the first two occurrences is disputed, cf. *ibid.,* 54.) and Wis 14:3. In striking contrast to the small number of Old Testament references, there are 255 occurrences of "Father" in the New Testament. Cf. F. Donahue, "The Spiritual Father in the Scriptures," *Abba: Guides to Wholeness and Holiness East and West* (ed. J. R. Sommerfeldt; Kalamazoo, MI: Cistercian, 1982) 3, 6.

2. Mary Daly, *Beyond God the Father: Towards a Philosophy of Women's Liberation* (Boston: Beacon, 1973). It is noteworthy that in a recent study of ancient Israelite women, Carol Meyers questions the validity of the term "patriarchal" for ancient Israelite (i.e. pre-monarcharchical) society. *Discovering Eve: Ancient Israelite Women in Context* (New York: Oxford University, 1988). For a survey of the recent major contributions to the discussion of patriarchalism-feminism in the Bible see Phyllis Trible, "Five Loaves and Two Fishes: Feminist Hermeneutics and Biblical Theology," *TS* 50 (1989), 279-295.

3. R. Hamerton-Kelly, 30.

4. Manfred Hauke in a study admirable in many other ways *Women and the Priesthood?: A Systematic Analysis in the Light of the Order of Creation and Redemption* (San Francisco: Ignatius, 1988) states (p. 222), "The accent in the father image is on authority." But this does not really reflect what is specific about the introduction of the father image into the Bible, as becomes clear in the passages we analyzed and especially in the teaching of Jesus. Authority is not absent but it is rooted in something more profound: God's love and election, his fatherly adoption of Israel.

5. Trible, "Five Loaves," points to Hos 11:9, "I will not destroy Ephraim again; for I am God and not man," where "man" translates the Hebrew *'ish*, meaning, she says, a male, instead of the generic *'adam* meaning "human." But this is mistaken, for *'ish* is also used generically at times, especially in passages (as here) contrasting man with God (Gen 32:29; Jgs 9:9, 13; 1 Sam 2:26; Is 2:11; 7:13, and especially Num 23:19, where it is parallel to *'adam*.) See also J. W. Miller, "Depatriarchalizing God in Biblical Interpretation: A Critique," *CBQ* 48 (1986), 622.

6. "For Orientals, the word 'father', as applied to God, thus encompasses, from earliest times, something of what the word 'mother' signifies among us." J. Jeremias, *The Prayer of Jesus* (Naperville, IL: Allenson, 1967), 95. My

30

confrere, Bernard Lee, has recently written (*The Galilean Jewishness of Jesus* [Mahwah NJ: Paulist, 1988], 38): "When God begins to be called Father in the Hebrew tradition, the system where the word father occurs in lived experience is a patriarchal system. It may be that the intended resemblance had to do with any good father's fidelity and care. Yet to call God 'father' unavoidably reinforces the patriarchal system and its functioning behavioral norms. The male father figure is the power figure." I hope our examination of texts amply demonstrates not only that the words "it may be that" can safely be dropped but that the texts actually counter the "power figure" in the direction of affectionate intimacy. Jesus will use the Father image actually to *subvert* much of the social system, including oppressive patriarchy, as we shall see. It is indeed unfortunate that some today read the "father" metaphor for an authority figure and nothing more, as a symbol for all that was wrong in the patriarchal system, without attempting to discover how the metaphor actually functioned within the culture. Hopefully, a more contextual reading of the texts will liberate us from such cultural chauvinism.

7. So Hauke, *Women in the Priesthood?,* 225, citing K. Leese, "The mother symbol inheres in the father symbol."

8. J. W. Miller, "Depatriarchalizing God," 610-611. See now his *Biblical Faith and Fathering: Why We Call God Father* (Mahwah NJ: Paulist, 1989).

9. Joachim Jeremias, 58, claims that *abba*, like *imma,* derives from children's speech ("Dada," "Mama"). James Barr ("Abba isn't 'Daddy,' " *JTS* 39 [1988] 28-47) has contested this claim, but he does admit (46) that "*abba* in Jesus' time belong to a familiar or colloquial register of language, as distinct from more formal and ceremonious usage."

10. It was a happy surprise for me when I asked our Indian novices the titles they used for "father." Since their maternal tongues were ancient tribal languages, the similarity to Hebrew and Aramaic was striking. In Kharia, the formal word is *Pita,* the informal, *Abba!* In Nepali, the formal is *Pita,* the informal *Baba,* or *Papa,* or *Ba.* In Tamil, the formal is *Pita* or *Thandai,* the informal, *Appa.* In Munda, *Abba* is used for both formal and informal. One of my graduate students, a Korean, tells me that his little daughter calls him "Abba," the familiar form in Korean equivalent to "Dad" or "Daddy."

11. Whether *all* the Greek usages of *father* on Jesus' lips are meant to translate *Abba* is disputed. G. Schrenk (*TDNT* 5:984-985), J. Jeremias (*Prayers,* 55-57) and G. Vermes (*Jesus and the World of Judaism* [Philadelphia: Fortress, 1984] 41), hold this position, while J. Barr (42-44) questions it. However, even if Jesus at times reverted to the formal word for "father," the *content* of his prayer and the behavioral implications he drew from it surely betray an unparalleled sense of intimacy with God.

12. Cf. Sandra M. Schneiders, *Women and the Word: The Gender of God in the New Testament and the Spirituality of Women* (New York: Paulist) 44-45. The single exception is Jesus' cry from the cross, "My God, my God, why have you forsaken me?" (Mk 15:34; Mt 27:46), but here Jesus is not inventing his own prayer but reciting the opening verse of Psalm 22, a psalm of trust and hope, which Jesus may have recited in its entirety. Luke drops this detail, replacing it with "Father, into your hands I commend my spirit" (Lk 23:46).

13. Vermes, 39. In the copious intertestamental literature God becomes increasingly transcendent and remote. Knowledge of him is mediated by the sacred books, the descent of angels, the gift of vision, or the journey of a seer through various heavens. Cf. J. H. Charlesworth, *The Old Testament Pseudepigrapha* 1 (Garden City: Doubleday, 1983) xxxi.

14. The witness of the Aramaic targums on this point is disputed. The targums were at first oral translations or paraphrases of the Scriptures composed at a time when Hebrew was no longer commonly spoken. The process began orally after the exile, but consigning the targums to writing did not occur until the first Christian centuries. There are in them two passages where the Hebrew "father" applied to God is rendered *Abba,* and one of them may not refer to God at all. In Malachi 2:10, "Have we not all the one Father (*abba*)? Has not the one God created us?", the word "father" may refer not to God but to Abraham or Jacob. The other is Psalm 89:27: "He shall say to me, 'You are my Father (*abba*), my God. . .' " Jeremias (60) maintains that since *abba*, without any possessive pronoun, had universally replaced *abhi* ("my father") in Aramaic by this time, and was used for "my father," "your father," etc., the possessive being understood from the context, the translator knew of no other way to render the expression than *abba*. Barr (43) adduces evidence from Aramaic documents at Qumran to contest this.

The overall silence of the Jewish documents is nonetheless striking. It is clear that of the many Old Testament titles available for God Jesus selected one that was not frequent but was, on the other hand, significantly relational, and used it in the familiar, colloquial form for his own prayer and as the keystone of his teaching.

15. Here and throughout this work I do not enter into the question of how much of Jesus' sayings-material is original with him, how much due to the development of Jesus' sayings in the period of oral tradition, and how much the work of the evangelist. In the matter of the fatherhood of God, there is general consensus that the development is continuous and consistent with the teaching of Jesus. See H. F. D. Sparks, "The Doctrine of the Divine Fatherhood in the Gospels," in *Studies in the Gospels* (Oxford: Blackwell, 1955), 259-260.

16. Begum Bilquis Sheik, with Richard Schneider, *I Dared to Call Him Father* (Lincoln VA: Chosen Books, 1978).

17. Though T. A. Smail's critique (*The Forgotten Father* [London: Hodder & Stoughton, 1980]) that the Father is neglected in the charismatic movement may be valid in some quarters, it certainly was not the case for me. It was a new discovery of the Father.

18. U.S. Bureau of the Census, *Statistical Abstract of the United States* (Washington, D.C.: Government Printing Office, 1989), 52.

19. W. M. Hardenbrook, *Missing from Action* (Nashville: T. Nelson, 1987), 90.

20. "For five-year-olds and over, the dominant symptom in both boys and girls was depression. In the absence of a father figure, children were sad, withdrawn and turned inward because they thought they were to blame for the breakup of the home." John Leo, "Single Parent, Double Trouble," *Time,* January 4, 1982, 81. For an earlier survey of social studies on the effects of fathering and the absence of father see R. A. Fein, "Research on Fathering: Social Policy and an Emergent Perspective," *Journal of Social Issues* 34 (1978), 122-135.

Chapter Two

IS ABBA ENOUGH?

When in Matthew's gospel Jesus teaches his disciples to pray "Our Father, *who art in heaven*," he implies that the heavenly Father is not just another Joseph. As a Jew, Jesus was keenly aware of the transcendence of God and that the intimacy he proclaimed could not possibly be of the same order as his intimacy with Joseph. Here we touch on an important theological issue which the logic of our presentation dictates we must deal with (though the reader is welcome to skip it or return to it later if he or she so desires). When the Scriptures use "Father" for God and when we in turn use it in worship or other contexts, the word is one from human language, and it inevitably evokes the universal experience of human fatherhood. But when we apply it to God, what happens to our language? What do we mean? God obviously does not have a body.

Nor does he have any of the other limitations we have. He is the creator of our being, and that is not the same thing as human fatherhood. And when we speak of God adopting us as his children by the grace of the Holy Spirit, we are speaking of a supernatural gift. If it impels us to cry, "Abba, Father!", what does that mean?

Analogy

Thomas Aquinas called this "stretching" of our language *analogy*. This manner of speaking is different from word use that is either *univocal* or *equivocal*. If I say, of a maple tree, "This is a *tree*," and of an oak, "This is a tree," the meaning of tree in both cases is the same. The meaning is univocal, i.e., the same. But when Shakespeare's Mercutio says, "Ask for me tomorrow and you shall find me a grave man," he is deliberately using *grave* in a double sense of "serious" and "tomb," and the humor of the line is that both completely different meanings accidentally meet in the same word. This is pure equivocation. It is the food of punsters.

Analogy is different. Two things can be completely different, yet there can be a perceptible likeness between them. If I say, "My dog is intelligent," I mean that in the dog world he shows a keenness that makes me think of human beings—which is one of the reasons dogs make good companions. There is a likeness, in other words, between my dog's intelligence and my own, even though he is not a rational animal, and no one expects me to send him to high school. Theologically, when we say "God is Father" we are not saying that God and our human father are the same kind of being (univocal); nor are we saying there is absolutely no likeness other than sound between the two words "father" (equivocal). We are saying that, while there is an infinite difference between God and human fathers, there is a likeness, a proportional likeness, which justifies our learning from the best of human fathers something of God's attitude to us.

Metaphor

Instead of analogy, most modern writers prefer the more common term *metaphor*.[1] Some modern philosophers of language would say that all our human speech is metaphorical. Certainly much of it is. Even such a simple statement as "the sun rises" is a metaphor, for the sun looks to us as if it is rising, whereas we know from science that the earth is spinning towards it. "You were an angel in church today," our mother may have told us when we behaved well—and maybe she called us something else when we didn't! Metaphors are the language not only of poets, novelists and songwriters. They are the way we describe and even shape our world. One of their functions is to enable us to describe the unknown or the unfamiliar by relating it to something known or familiar.

The power of a metaphor comes from its partial truth. No one image can say everything about an object (you were not *just* an angel in church!), but it says one, or a few things, graphically, movingly. If I had to add all the things I omitted in my metaphor to assure its "complete" truth, my sentence would die the death of a thousand qualifications. If a metaphor were hailed into court to take an oath, it would have to say, "I swear to tell the truth, but not the whole truth." That is why every metaphor is limited. And certainly, in describing God, no one metaphor is adequate.

That means not only that metaphors can be multiplied in order to describe God (Hindus and Muslims speak of the "thousand names of God") but that even the metaphors we use for God need to be understood without the limitations they have in normal human speech. Thus, if "father," as we saw in previous chapter, is an extremely rich metaphor given us by Jesus, there are certain limitations of the term which we should *not* transfer when applying it to God: (1) "Maleness" should not be transferred, to the exclusion of "femininity," when using the metaphor "father" of God. Our examination of the biblical texts already pointed in this direction. St. Gregory Nazianzen took the matter for granted in the fourth century:

> We have to regard it indispensable to apply our earthly words to the divinity in a metaphorical sense, especially those that for us concern parenting. Do you imagine that God is the masculine sex because we call him God [*Theos*, masculine gender in Greek] and Father?[2]

(2) Its cultural "baggage," in this case the limitations and the abuses of the patriarchal system, should not be transferred (in fact, we saw that the Old Testament father metaphor, applied to God, was already itself countering negative patriarchal power imagery, a direction Jesus reinforced); and (3) We should be conscious of our tendency to load "Father" with our negative experiences when we apply it to God.

Is "Father" Oppressive?

The points just discussed about "transfer" are crucial in the contemporary feminist debate over the appropriateness of "Father" as a name of God. Some claim that not only is the metaphor limited; it is oppressive and destructive:

The destructiveness of the metaphor ["Father"] is that it easily supports patriarchy, a fundamental denial of the equality of women and men. The continuing exclusion of women from power structures in some traditions is a religious example. The lower wages paid women for performing the same work as men is a secular example, but one that is often pitched under the "sacred canopy" of religious reasons . . . Will Goddess the Mother become a metaphor alongside God the Father? Will the Parenthood of God replace the Fatherhood of God?[3]

What is to be said about this correlation of the oppression of women with the prayer metaphor "Father"? This requires a closer look at the dynamics of metaphor.

Certain metaphors have a power to touch us deeply. Martin Luther King's refrain, "I have a dream," in his famous civil rights speech moved people like a rallying drumbeat. Because of their power, metaphors can either build or destroy, they can either heal or hurt. And that is because metaphors have their histories. And we have our histories. And when a metaphor with its history meets us with our history, two worlds are meeting.

In the previous chapter I discussed how during one period of my life the words "Our father" had a painful resonance in my heart. My world, my experience, my personal history, my "road" was meeting the road of Christianity at the signpost "father," and the experience was not comfortable. Without realizing it, I was emotionally "stuck" there for years. I was carrying a lot of baggage about my "father" that I had to unload before I could move ahead. Was there something wrong with the sign? Had collective Christianity beaten a wrong path, that we should get stuck here? Should I have demanded that the sign be changed? Or was this the challenge that I needed to face about my own world and my own history?

Since metaphors originate in a limited human culture and experience, they will sometimes be perceived as carrying "baggage" with them when they are heard or used by persons in another time, place, or culture. This baggage can be enriching; it can sometimes be entrapping. When, for example, as a Christian I hear the phrase "liberation of the oppressed" from the mouth of a Marxist, I may welcome it because Jesus used the same term to describe his mission (Luke 4:18). But for the Marxist I might soon discover the term means violent revolution and the victory of the party at any cost. Does that mean I should scrap the term "liberation"? I could, of course, do so. But it would be simpler for me to consciously unburden the metaphor of its Marxist baggage and indicate the Christian meaning by the way I use the term and live out its meaning. When we take a metaphor from one context and apply it to another, we need to decide consciously how much of the accompanying baggage we want, how much we don't. And especially when examining scriptural metaphors, we should ask ourselves whether the baggage we perceive comes from the original context or whether in fact it comes from *our* cultural context and the limitations of our personal experience.

Now there is no question that the culture of Jesus was patriarchal. There were a lot of good things about that culture, but by today's standards there were some practices that many would call oppressive, particularly in the role assigned to women. But was the word "Father" for God to blame?

There is, obviously, a correlation between the father-hood of God and human fatherhood. The very use of the same word indicates that. Ephesians 3:14 says, moreover, that God the Father is the one after whom every *patria* is named. The Greek word *patria* is often translated "family," but it really means "fatherhood." Instead of working upward from the human analogy, this Ephesians text works downward: the fatherhood of God gives reality and substance to all human fatherhood. A consequence of this is that human fathers are not autocrats but should model themselves after God the Father not merely in their specific parenting role but in strong, tender and compassionate love with which God as Father is portrayed in the Bible. A second consequence is that "Father" as a title for God should not be blamed for all the misuse, abuse, or nonuse of the father's role in human history. In fact, in Mt 23:8-9 Jesus uses the title "Father" for God as a means of relativizing human paternity and subverting the oppressive claims of the human patriarchal system.[4] For him the word "Abba" meant, among other things, a new and revolutionary way to relate to women. If the word "Father" has been used by others at times to support the oppression of women, that can only come from a complete misunderstanding of the biblical texts and of Jesus' teaching about *abba*.[5] Jesus' use of the divine father metaphor to proclaim liberation and communion shows that the meaning of a metaphor and its behavioral consequences are not imposed by the metaphor's original context, but derive from how one chooses to hear and use that metaphor in the new context. Hence, it is not the religious metaphor itself which is the telling factor in confirming the status quo or in changing it, but how it is behaviorly applied. If the title "father" has been behaviorly abused, the same could hold for any title given to God, even the most gentle and maternal.

Thus it is important to distinguish three different levels when we speak of a metaphor like "Father" applied to God:

(1) *The level of metaphor as language.* When a person speaks or writes a metaphor, he or she carves out a meaning from human language, but the metaphor itself is only a roadsign, an arrow pointing in a given direction. When, in the journey of that metaphor through history, paths diverge and new applications of the metaphor are proposed, it is imperative to discover which paths may have been intended by the originator of the metaphor, which not. That we have tried to do in our study above.

(2) *The sociopolitical implications of the metaphor.* These are chosen by the persons who use the metaphor to support certain political or social aims. Thus some may have used "father" to support an oppressive patriarchy, but this goes obviously against the intention of Jesus, who drew quite different sociopolitical consequences from the metaphor. Others, following the example of Jesus, used the word "Father" for liberation. If a false path has been taken, it is the path that needs to be rejected, not the metaphor.[6]

(3) *The role of the metaphor in personal transformation.* For a person who had a strong, bonding relationship with his/her father, the transfer of "father" to God will, in most cases, be delightful. For the fatherless it may be more difficult but surely not impossible if there have been other healthy father figures in one's life. For those whom the metaphor strikes negatively, the difficulty may signal unresolved conflicts in that individual's personal

history. This can lead to healing, integration and growth. (The same could be said for the "mother" metaphor as well, since it alerts one to one's history of relationship with one's mother.)

Other Names for God?

After this long discussion occasioned by the question of whether "Father" is "oppressive," we return to the question of the limitations of metaphor. Since the name "Father" does not exhaust the mystery of God, it is certainly possible to use other names, as indeed the Bible itself does. In recent years, however, largely due to the feminist movement and the concern for inclusive language, other names have been proposed not as complements but as replacements of the word *Father*. Because the name is seen to evoke not only origin of life and, in the Abba form, intimacy, but also maleness, some translators of the Lord's prayer have suggested "inclusive" substitutes such as "Our Parent," or "Our Creator" or "Our Friend" or "Source of all Being." Clearly, these names are cheap and deceptive substitutes for the richness we have just seen in Jesus' understanding of "Abba."[7] What child, on returning home from school, says "Hi, parent"?[8] And "Creator," though certainly true of the supreme being, does not at all convey the new meaning in God-consciousness revealed by Jesus. Muslims too believe in God the creator. Whereas "Father" lends itelf both to the mutual relations within the Trinity and to the sharing of that supernatural relationship with his children *ad extra*, "Creator" deals only with God's giving being to those outside himself. "Source of all being" falls in the same category—a philosophical term that has no Trinitarian reference. "Friend" can certainly lay no claim to equivalency for *Abba*. I have many friends; I have only one Father. Nor do I have to be a male to revel in my daddy's love. Instead of being inclusive, the proposed alternatives end up being exclusive of the heart of Jesus' revelation. It should, of course, be obvious that replacing "Father" with a neuter title depersonalizes God and makes intimacy impossible.

God as Mother?

Others, aware of the rich content of "Father" but also claiming its limitation, have suggested adding the maternal title, so that we would say, "Our Father and Mother." The suggestion has the advantage of keeping "Father." And if it is legitimate to add other other titles in our prayers, to say, for example, "Our Father and King," "Our Father and Creator," "Our Father and Friend," all of which can claim a biblical basis, why might we not similarly add the title "Mother"?

There are, in fact, more Old Testament precedents than one might expect showing God with a maternal face. Aside from the texts associating a maternal function with the father image, which we saw in the previous chapter, there are several others not so connected: "As one whom his mother comforts, so I will comfort you" (Is 66:13 RSV). "Can a mother forget her infant, be without tenderness for the child of her womb? Even should she forget, I will never forget you" (Is 49:15). In Is 42:14 through the prophet the Lord describes his imminent action in birthing terms: "For a long time I have held my peace, I have kept still and restrained myself; now I will cry out like a woman in travail, I will gasp and pant" (RSV).

The image of the mother bird appears in various ways.

44

Repeatedly the Psalmist speaks of finding refuge in the shadow of God's wings (Pss 17:8; 36:7; 57:2; 63:7). In the first creation account, the spirit of God broods or hovers over the waters (Gen 1:2). The verb can evoke the bird's patient waiting for the eggs to hatch or, more likely, the hovering by which she encourages the fledglings to fly from the nest. The image appears in Is 31:5: "Like hovering birds, so the LORD of hosts shall shield Jerusalem; to protect and deliver, to spare and rescue it." In this case, the mother bird hovers over the nest to protect her young. In his lament over Jerusalem Jesus used the image of the bird or hen extending her wings in welcome and protection: "Jerusalem, Jerusalem, you who kill the prophets and stone those sent to you, how many times I yearned to gather your children as a hen gathers her brood under her wings, but you were unwilling!" (Lk 13:34)

Finally, God's wisdom in the Old Testament is at times personified as a woman (Prov 1:20-33; 8:1-36).

> Wisdom has built her house,
>> she has set up her seven column;
> She has dressed her meat, mixed her wine,
>> yes, she has spread her table.
> She has sent out her maidens; she calls
>> from the heights out over the city:
> "Let whoever is simple turn in here;
>> to him who lacks understanding, I say,
> Come, eat of my food,
>> and drink of the wine I have mixed! (Prov 9:1-5)

This feminine personification of wisdom has the advantage of balancing the strong commands of the law and the threats of the prophets with the sweet invitation, the attractiveness, the holy seduction of God's truth—

compared in Scripture with the sweetness of honey (Prov 24:13-14; Sir 24:19). Thus Solomon says, "Her I loved and sought after from my youth; I sought to take her for my bride, and I was enamored of her beauty" (Wis 8:2). Or again, he says that she is the mother of all good things (Wis 7:12). The images of mother and bride are combined in Sir 15:2: "Motherlike she will meet him, like a young bride she will embrace him, . . . "

It is significant, however, that in the wisdom texts, though wisdom is said to dwell with God, she is something distinct from God (7:25-26; 8:3). And thus we must conclude that despite these feminine images, nowhere in the Old Testament is God addressed as "Mother" or with any other distinctly female title.

The same is true in the New Testament. It has been suggested that the Holy Spirit is the feminine element in the Trinity.[9] This cannot be argued from gender either in Greek or Hebrew, since the Greek *pneuma* is neuter and the Hebrew *ruah* is sometimes masculine, sometimes feminine. But it is true that what are generally considered feminine attributes are often associated with the spirit of God. The spirit that inheres in wisdom has many feminine traits (Wis 7:2-8:2). The "spirit of God" that hovers like a mother bird over the waters of creation (Gen 1:2) recurs in the baptism of Jesus in the image of the dove (Mt 3:16). Still, just as in the Old Testament God is never explicitly addressed as "Mother," so in the New Testament neither the Father, nor Jesus nor the Holy Spirit is so addressed.

The Goddesses

Why this reluctance? Is it that the culture of the Old Testament and of Jesus was patriarchal? If it were that simple, then all other patriarchal societies would have limited their god-language to a single, male title for God. But such was not the case. Israel was surrounded by peoples who worshipped goddesses. Canaan and Syria had Anath, Astarte and Asherah. The Babylonians worshipped Ishtar. These, along with Cybele, the Great Mother of Phrygia, were all fertility goddesses. Their worship was widespread and popular even in Israel, despite repeated prophetic condemnations. Excavations like the one I was on at Gezer in 1966 repeatedly unearthed the goddess, pregnant and with exaggerated breasts and genitals, in a clay image that could be held in the hand of the worshipper, presumably, for a woman devotee, giving the promise of successful conception. Along with Baal, her brother-consort, Anath was the goddess who gave fertility to the land, livestock and the race. The annual dying of Baal and his rising through Anath's intervention was the Canaanites' way of celebrating the cycle of the seasons, the death of nature in winter and its resurgence in spring. The worship of the fertility goddesses also involved ritual prostitution. But Canaanite society, for all its exaltation of female goddesses, was no less patriarchal than Israel, and its worship of woman as object of fertility did nothing to elevate her dignity, but on the contrary focused only on the sexual, generative dimension of her role.

Israel's great struggle with the fertility gods and goddesses is recorded most brilliantly in the books of Kings. What was threatened in the first place was not the masculinity of Israel's God (the name Yahweh, "I am," has nothing to do with sex) but the strict monotheism of Yahwistic religion. It is true that the substitute *Adonai* means "Lord," and Israel worshipped Yahweh under the

47

image of King and other masculine titles. But the fight against the gods and goddesses of Canaan was not a fight to defend a male god against female goddesses. It was a fight to maintain the one God against the many. Adding a goddess' name to that of Yahweh, or making Yahweh androgynous, would have been an inadmissable compromise of monotheistic Yahwism.[10]

There was more involved, of course, than a mere theoretical monotheism. The fertility goddesses were identified with the processes of nature, with mother earth, with the cycle of the eternal return.[11] Israel's God was, on the contrary, the God of history, of intervention, of free choice and free action, a God of redemption and liberation. And he was not part of the process of nature. He was the author of nature, the creator—a theme most lyrically sung by Second Isaiah. There were, of course, agricultural feasts in Israel, but these were given a historical reinterpretation as celebrations of the great deeds of Yahweh. Add to this the strong ethical thrust of the covenant and the prophets and you have ample reason for resistance to the fertility cults of Canaan.

What was at issue was, in the last analysis, the *transcendence* of God. Could not a monotheistic mother title instead of the father title have served as well? This question goes beyond mere exegetical science. The comparative study of religions, which we have touched on only briefly, sheds helpful light here. It appears established that the father image lends itself more readily to the dimension of transcendence, the maternal more to immanence.[12] Maternal images bespeak closeness, connectedness to the earth and creation, and thus more easily lend themselves to pantheism. While pantheism proclaims an immanence without transcendence, the Judaeo-Christian worldview holds to an immanence that presupposes transcendence, and this is expressed and preserved in various ways in the tradition, one of which is the fatherhood of God, enriched but not replaced by maternal images of closeness. The father image, of course, runs the risk of overemphasizing the distance between God and his people; but the prophets preferred to overcome this danger by incorporating maternal imagery into the father title than to run the all-too-present risk of identifying Israel's God with the processes of nature by using a maternal title. Jesus himself sought to express and convey the intimacy of God *within* the tradition of God's fatherhood.

With the Apostles and Thereafter

The struggle for monotheism continued in the age of the apostles. Paul met it head on at Ephesus in the cult of Artemis, the fertility goddess whose gigantic temple was one of the wonders of the ancient world. Under the name Diana, she was also worshipped in Rome. Later, according to the church Fathers Irenaeus and Justin, Simon Magus, the father of gnosticism, had an associate by the name of Helena, "the Mother of all," who was worshipped as a goddess, though in fact she was a prostitute from Tyre.[13] Elsewhere among the gnostics, the Holy Spirit is identified as a woman,[14] the divine mother[15], or, according to the gnostic Acts of Thomas 111, as the "mother, Queen of the East." One text describes God as "the Father, the Mother, and the Son."[16] More pertinently, the God of Israel, the Creator, was not really the source of all being; he was a demiurge begotten by a divine "mother," who is often depicted as the female wisdom who fell away from the perfection and praise of the transcendent God.[17] And even the humanity created by her offspring, the God of Israel, was superior to its creator.[18] But the ultimate God remained unknown and unknowable. The "eternal silence," the "unknown" of gnosticism is a long way from the *Abba* of Jesus.[19] Though it appeared to exalt woman by promoting her to ecclesiastical offices, gnostic belief that the material world is evil led to an ascetical radicalism and rejection of sexuality on the one hand and, on the other, sexual license, since what one did in the material body was of no consequence.

> Gnosticism had, as it were, a place for woman in heaven as participating in creation, and a place in hell as the temptress responsible for man's imprisonment in sexuality. It had, however, no place for her as a person, as a human being on earth. It was therefore fundamentally opposed to marriage as a lifelong covenant between two persons. It is not surprising, therefore, that the early church was profoundly suspicious of all gnostic tendencies, and especially of any attempt to use feminine or maternal symbols for God.[20]

The nineteenth century abolitionists, following the lead of Jesus and the gospels, appealed to the fatherhood of God as a mandate for the freeing of slaves. Martin Luther King, who struggled for the equality of "all God's children," used the fatherhood of God to urge confidence and perseverance in the struggle for human rights.[21] Some twentieth century feminists, rejecting the name Father for God, would strangely suggest a return to the nature goddesses of the fertility cults, or to gnosticism, as a path for the liberation of women, when in fact historically those cults demeaned them. If history has anything to teach us, getting rid of "Father" for God and feminizing it or neutering it will do nothing to elevate the status of women—in fact, it could be a distraction from the social and political fields where the battle must be fought.[22] I lived for six years in the Hindu kingdom of Nepal, where goddesses were as numerous and as ubiquitous as gods, where the great mother-goddess Durga was celebrated in the chief festival of the year, where the busiest intersection in the capital city was dominated by a yellow billboard proclaiming in bright red letters, in Nepali and English, "Mother and Motherland are greater than heaven." Yet all of this had no perceptible influence on the social uplift of women. Metaphors can reinforce oppression or launch liberation—or be socially neutral because they are never used to challenge the sociopolitical structure of the culture. The meaning of a metaphor is therefore only in part a *given*. Its meaning is not imposed; it is chosen.

Feminine Metaphors in Later Centuries

We have seen that the climate of polytheism, nature religions and gnosticism, plus the strong tradition of *Abba* going back to Jesus, explains the early church's resistance to using feminine titles for God. Yet the postbiblical tradition knows occasionally of feminine metaphors used, as they were in the Old Testament, for the Lord in his outward relation to the work of creation and redemption. The dating and the interpretation of the *Odes of Solomon* is disputed. The second century work may be gnostic but it may also have been a hymnbook used in the Christian liturgy of baptism. In 8:14 Christ speaks: "My own breasts I prepared for them, that they might drink my holy milk and live by it." J.H. Bernard gathers impressive evidence that "the representation of the Word as Milk, and the interpretation of Milk as the Flesh of the Word, were current in the second and third centuries." But J. H. Charlesworth notes that in the New Testament already "milk" and "word" were linked conceptually, and he refers to 1 Cor 3:1-2 and 1 Pt 2:2.[23] If this is the sense, then the metaphor would be a way of portraying Jesus as feeding the newly baptized with his word. We know from other sources that in some early liturgies the newly baptized were given a cup of milk to drink.[24] In Ode 19 the breast imagery is applied to the Father. The same tradition appears in Clement of Alexandria who writes, about the year 180:

> The Word is everything to the child, both father teacher and nurse . . . The nutriment is the milk of the Father . . . and the Word alone supplies us children with the milk of love, and only those who suck at this breast are truly happy. For this reason, seeking is called sucking; to those infants who seek the Word, the Father's loving breasts supply milk.[25]

Centuries later the mystic Julian of Norwich, herself influenced by the writings of William of Thierry in this matter (d.1148), reflecting on the activity of God in creation and re-creation, can say, "God rejoices that he is our Father; God rejoices that he is our mother."[26] St. Anselm, following Jesus' own example, addresses the Son thus: "And you, Jesus, are you not also a mother? Are you not the mother who like a hen gathers her chickens under her wings?"[27] There is evidence of the existence of a devotion to "Jesus our Mother" in the Middle Ages.[28]

Jesus is presented as Wisdom in some New Testament passages (Mt 11:28-30; 1 Cor 1:24). Though neither

Matthew nor Paul exploit the feminine implications of this identification, St. Louis de Montfort's favorite title for Jesus is *La Sagesse Eternelle et Incarnée* (Eternal and Incarnate Wisdom), which forces him to refer often to Jesus as *elle* (she)! The English translators of Montfort's works felt it "improper" to call Jesus *she*![29]

To the Holy Spirit as well the maternal aspects of God's work have been attributed. If the genders of the noun *spirit* in the Hebrew and Greek bibles hardly permit such attribution, as we have seen, certainly many of the ways the spirit is described in the bible suggest the fittingness of this attribution — from the bird hovering over the waters of creation in Genesis 1:2 to the dove hovering over Jesus at his baptism. Recent scholarship has shown how rich the early Syriac tradition is in this feminine imagery for the Holy Spirit, though the influence of the Greeks and especially the concern for orthodoxy in the face of gnosticism apparently led to a later abandoning of certain ambiguous terminology, as, for example the image of the Holy Spirit as Jesus' divine mother—a point to which we shall devote particular attention momentarily.

Though these usages of feminine imagery are striking, it is rather clear, from the mainstream of the tradition, that such feminine attributions were just that—attributions legitimized by the Scriptures' occasional similar practice and by the understanding that even such a title as "Abba" in God was never intended to be limited to maleness. Some feminist theologians have sought support in the Angelus address of Pope John Paul I of September 10, 1978, in which it is maintained he said, "While God is indeed our Father, he is our mother even more,"[30] or "God is Father, but above all, God is Mother."[31] Unfortunately, this is an inaccurate translation of the Italian, particularly if the implication is that God is more mother that father. Commenting on Is 49:15, the Pope said, *E papà; più ancora è madre*, which the official translation renders, "He is our father; even more he is our mother," which simply indicates, in keeping with the biblical tradition, that the limitations of the father metaphor are completed by the maternal.[32] Hauke correctly observes: "He most certainly did not maintain that God is more mother than father."[33]

Not just Like Jesus but With Him: Beyond Metaphor

Up to this point we have been speaking about Jesus' choice of a human analogy or metaphor to speak of God. And for the most part we have not differentiated the persons of the Trinity, for even those traits "attributed" to one of the persons because of a certain fittingness, in reality belong to all three. God as the one God, Father, Son and Holy Spirit, is *like,* if beyond, the best of human fathers. But that does not exhaust the mystery. The best is yet to come! Our adoption by God in Jesus makes us real "sharers in the divine nature" (2 Peter 1:4). When Jesus says ". . . go to my brothers and tell them, I am going to my Father and your Father, to my God and your God" (John 20:17), the base of comparison is not human fatherhood at all but Jesus' own relationship with his Father, and that means we are in some way introduced into the Trinitarian intimacy of the Son with the Father, first person of the Trinity. That is what Jesus' discourse at the Last Supper is all about. And that is not "just a comparison," but a reality, as 1 John 3:1 makes clear:

See what love the Father has bestowed on us that we may be called the children of God. Yet so we are.

54

If we want to know what calling God "Abba" means, then, in the last analysis we are to look not to our human fathers but to Jesus' relationship with his heavenly Father, and by "Father" in this case we mean the first person of the Trinity. From that viewpoint, even the category "metaphor" is inadequate, for our relationship with the Father is not just *like* Jesus' relationship with the Father; it is an actual, if created, participation in that relationship.[34] That relationship is utterly unique and transcendent, and therefore a mystery. Now if Jesus chose the word "Father" to express it, then that choice belongs to the uniqueness of Jesus' revelation. We may certainly say that the mystery transcends the limits of our human word "father," as the Bible already intimated by enriching it with complementary images, including the feminine. But to suggest changing the name itself is to call into question the very structure of Jesus' revelation.

"Metaphors" within the Trinity

Thus the problem becomes delicate, in fact crucial, when we leave the realm of "attributions" and begin to discuss the proper relations within the Trinity itself (*ad intra*). For there, the first person of the Trinity is the source, the second the begotten, and the third proceeds from the first through the second. Therefore to call the Holy Spirit "Mother" within the Trinity is a highly confusing and contradictory metaphor. And even to speak of the Holy Spirit as the divine mother of Jesus in the mystery of the Incarnation could easily lead to the conclusion that Jesus proceeds from the Holy Spirit.[35]

"Father," on the other hand, is the tradition's revealed way of describing in human language the sourcing or "parenting" relationship of the first person of the Trinity in regard to the Second, the Word. For this reason, some have suggested the combined title "Father-Mother" (i.e. "Parent") for this relationship, and there is even some justification in tradition for this, as the council of Toledo in 675 spoke of the second Person being born of the "womb of the Father."[36] Now, obviously "Father," used alone, is not meant to convey maleness. The problem with adding "Mother" as metaphor for the first Person is that the addition seems to *assume* what the tradition never assumed, i.e., that "Father" *does* mean maleness, and therefore the addition appears to do exactly the opposite of what it is intended to do. The least we can say is that insisting that "Father" does not mean maleness (a tradition going back explicitly at least to St. John Damascene) is as valid an option as adding "Mother," particularly since in our human experience it is difficult to envision one person being both father and mother.

The second Person of the Trinity, described as "the Word" in the prologue of John and elsewhere, is fittingly called the "Son," not primarily because of the internal relations within the Trinity, but because it was the Second Person alone who became incarnate, and he did so as a male. This is a "scandal" which has led some radical feminists to abandon Christianity altogether. Yet it is seen by other Christian feminists as part of God's design to redeem oppressive patriarchy by entering and subverting it from within, as a male, Jesus having lived and proclaimed as integrated, balanced, equalizing brother-sisterhood, the ideal of authentic feminism.[37] Whether or not that hypothesis can be sustained, it is rather obvious that to focus only on Jesus' maleness rather than on his becoming *one of us* is a dichotomizing approach to the economy of salvation, and it especially neglects the intimate and exalted role of his feminine associate, whether this be the church as *mystery* or Mary as mother. But more of this later.

Polyvalent Meanings

Most of our uses of "Father" for God have an ambiguity about them, because it is not clear whether we are speaking of God as the one supreme being (and therefore all the persons of the Trinity at once), the God to whom Jesus too, viewed uniquely from the viewpoint of his human nature, relates (God *ad extra*); or the first Person of the Trinity to whom Jesus in his divine personhood, relates (God *ad intra*). This ambiguity, however, is the ambiguity not of confusion but of mystery, because by grace God is not only our source of divine life as the One God, but by the same grace of adoption we are caught up into the Trinitarian relationships themselves, as we relate to the first person of the Trinity through Jesus in the Spirit. Thus in our God-language, especially in the liturgy, we seem to be saying both things at the same time when we use the word "Father."

Could "Mother" have the same polyvalence? Theoretically, yes. But, since our relationship with God is in and with the Incarnate Jesus, the warp and woof of the historical economy of God, particularly the mystery of the Incarnation, could become unraveled. It is in and through the Incarnation that we are brought into the life of the Trinity, so that as a matter of fact for us Incarnation and Trinity are inseparably joined. And in that inseparable fusion of mysteries, Jesus has an earthly mother who is not God. And she is not merely mother of his humanity but, as the Council of Ephesus insisted, *theotokos,* human mother of the second person of the

57

Trinity. Is it surprising that the gnostics who posited a divine mother for Jesus despised the material dimension of his incarnation in Mary, to say nothing of humanness in general? To introduce another "Mother" would immeasurably confuse the symbols and the reality of our Trinitarian-Incarnational faith. It is a heavy price to pay for tampering with the divine names given to us in the sources of divine revelation.

A Conclusion and an Unopened Door

It should be obvious, from all we have see thus far, that the term "Father," though limited as every human image and concept is, belongs to the historical core of divine revelation. Understood in its biblical sense, it is essential and irreplaceable as the address Jesus gave us for God. It can be complemented with a vast number of metaphors, including the feminine. But the church's public worship, in which the law of praying reflects the law of faith (*lex orandi, lex credendi*), cannot abandon it without dismantling the heart of Jesus' revelation.

But does it follow that the feminine is less important, less essential to the Catholic faith or to its appropriation by the church and the individual? I think not. For there are voices in the tradition that we have not yet heard. This leads us to retrace our steps through the historical trajectory of revelation to see whether, in our haste to find feminine imagery used either of God in himself or in his external works, we have missed something. Like foreign prospectors, with tools of another world, we have mined that tradition and not found it wanting in feminine imagery. But if we now follow the Bible on its own terrain, it is just possible that we may find there a richer lode.

The Feminine as Response and Instrumentality

When we examine the *preferred* mode taken by the tradition, we see the feminine symbolism used liberally for the human response to the initiative of God and, particularly in the later tradition, as mediator of God's life-giving power. The response-dimension appears first in the prophet Hosea, who describes the covenant as Yahweh's espousing the people, his bride (Hos 2). This espousal has all the pathos of a love affair, and it extends to fertility of land and cattle:

> So I will allure her;
>> I will lead her into the desert
>> and speak to her heart.
>
> From there I will give her the vineyards she had,
>> and the valley of Achor as a door of hope
>> [the valley of entrance to the promised land].
>
> She shall respond there as in the days of her youth,
>> when she came up from the land of Egypt.
>
> On that day, says the LORD,
> She shall call me "My husband,"
>> and never again "My baal."
>
> I will make a covenant for them on that day,
>> with the beasts of the field,
>
> With the birds of the air,
>> and with the things that crawl on the ground.
>
> Bow and sword and war
>> I will destroy from the land,
>> and I will let them take their rest in security.
>
> I will espouse you to me forever:
>> I will espouse you in right [sedeq] and in justice [mishpat],
>> in love [hesed] and mercy [rehamim];

59

I will espouse you in fidelity [emunah],
and you shall know the LORD.

On that day I will respond, says the LORD;
I will respond to the heavens [that ask for clouds],
and they shall respond to the earth [that asks for
rain]
The earth shall respond to the grain, and wine, and
oil [that ask for fertile soil],... (Hos 2:16-24)

This imagery is continued by Jeremiah (2:2) and developed into a lengthy allegory by Ezekiel (16:1-63). The Canticle of Canticles is probably a collection of love songs, but it is open to an allegorical interpretation as Yahweh's love for his people and their—the bride's—response. That interpretation has been common in the tradition.

The male deities of Israel's neighbors had their female consorts. Israel's God had no other consort than Israel herself, whom he chose to espouse in covenant. The result was that all his passionate, spousal love focused upon his people.

This motif of passionate, spousal love becomes the inspiration for much of the mystical tradition in which it is the primary model for the union of the individual soul with the Lord. St. John of the Cross is the outstanding mystic in the west to have exploited the imagery.

Inasmuch as the capital city, Jerusalem, is metonomy for the people, it soon became fashionable to refer to her in feminine terms. In the Lamentations this occurs no less than 17 times. She is daughter Zion (1:6; 2:1, 4:8, 10), virgin daughter Zion (21:13), daughter Judah (2:5), virgin daughter Judah (1:15), daughter Jerusalem (2:13, 15), daughter of my people (2:11; 4:3, 6, 10) and widow (1:1). In the New Testament this symbolism is carried over to the church, the bride, of whom Jesus is the bridegroom (Mk 2:21; John 3:29; Mt 25:1-13; Eph 5:25-27; Rev 21:2, 9).

But Jerusalem is also mother. Cities in the ancient world were often called mother, but there was in Jerusalem a topographical reason for the title. Mounts Zion and Moriah, divided by the Tyropean valley, easily suggested a mother's breasts. In postexilic Judaism, Jerusalem was hailed as mother not only of the present generation (Ps 87:5) but of the new people of God yet to be born:

> Before she comes to labor, she gives birth;
> Before the pains come upon her, she safely delivers
>   a male child.
> Who ever heard of such a thing, or saw the like?
> Can a country be brought forth in one day, or a
>   nation be born in a single moment?
> Yet Zion is scarcely in labor when she gives birth
>   to her children.
> Shall I bring a mother to the point of birth, and yet
>   not let her child be born? says the LORD.
> Or shall I who allow her to conceive, yet close her
>   womb? says your God.
> Rejoice with Jerusalem and be glad because of her,
>   all you who love her;
> Exult, exult with her, all you who were mourning
>   over her!
> Oh, that you may suck fully of the milk of her
>   comfort,
> That you may nurse with delight at her abundant
>   breasts!
> For thus says the LORD:

61

> Lo, I will spread prosperity over her like a river,
>   and the wealth of nations like an overflowing
>   torrent.
> As nurslings, you shall be carried in her arms,
>   and fondled in her lap;
> As a mother comforts her son, so will I comfort
>   you;
>   in Jerusalem you shall find your comfort.
>
> (Is 66:7-13)

Not only does this text recall the maternal action of God ("As a mother comforts her son, so will I comfort you"); nor does it merely present the city of Jerusalem in the role of mother (throughout). *Jerusalem mediates the maternal love of God*: "Shall *I* bring a mother to the point of birth . . . shall *I* allow her to conceive, yet close her womb? . . . As a mother comforts her son, so will *I* comfort you; in *Jerusalem* you shall find your comfort." The comforting, like the birthing, is the work both of God and of Jerusalem, or more precisely, of God *through* the instrumentality of the city, Mother Zion.

In the New Testament these two pivotal functions of the feminine image, response and instrumentality, find their fulfillment beyond expectations in Mary, the Mother of Jesus. It will be the thesis of this book that Mary by her faith embodies the response to the revealing, enfleshing Word of God, and by her motherhood of the elect she mediates the maternal love of the Father. Mary reveals the maternal face of God.

NOTES

1. In discussing the divine names, i.e., the appropriateness of our human language for God, Aquinas also speaks of metaphor. He understands it in a restricted sense of words that because of their limited *mode* of signification apply primarily to creatures and only by way of similitude to God (e.g., "God is my rock"); whereas other predicates not necessarily implying limitation (e.g., "God is good, wise, living, etc.") apply primarily to God because they belong to his essence, even though they are first drawn from human experience of those traits. The latter he understands as proper analogy. *Summa Theol.* I, q. 13, arts. 3 & 6.

2. Gregory of Nazianzen, *Orat.* 31:7, *Sources Chrtiennes* 250, 289.

3. B. Lee, 117.

4. I do not want to suggest that Jesus eliminated authority from God by his use of *Abba*. The gospels make it abundantly clear that the Father has divine authority and that he exercises it. It is not, however, an "oppresssive" authority, save perhaps for those who are ideologically committed to a society and a church in which all authorities are banned and "equality" means submission to nobody.

5. The biblical scholar Celine Mangan, in a popular book on prayer, *Can We Still Call God "Father"?* (Wilmington DL: Michael Glazier, 1984) 9-42, has a helpful discussion on how the image of "father" is heard differently in different cultural situations and how the biblical image of "father" needs to be rediscovered in its original rich and comprehensive meanings. "It is possible for God to be experienced as paternal without being experienced as a patriarch," S. Schneiders, *Women and the Word* (New York: Paulist, 1986), 15.

6. "Jesus' address to God as 'Abba' cannot be construed as a revelation of the maleness of God nor as a divine model for human patriarchy," Schneiders, 49.

7. I do not mean to suggest that the other titles mentioned are false, only that when they are used to *replace* "Father" they are inadequate and, in fact, misleading.

8. J. W. Fowler has shown how central the early relationships of the child with both father and mother are to the development of a mature understanding of God. Neutering God or otherwise removing the specific parental title would make difficult, if not impossible, the transfer from the intimate *known* to the intimate *unknown. Stages of Faith: Psychology of Human Development and Quest for Meaning* (New York: Harper and Row, 1981) and *Becoming Adult, Becoming Christian: Adult Development of Christian Faith* (New York: Harper and Row, 1981).

9. See D. L. Gelpi, *The Divine Mother: A Trinitarian Theology of the Holy Spirit* (Lanham MD: University Press of America, 1984); Y. M. J. Congar, "The Motherhood of God and the Femininity of the Holy Spirit" in *I Believe in the Holy Spirit* III (New York: Seabury, 1983) 155-164.

10. In the preface I noted how Genesis 1:26 portrays the male and female as created in the image and likeness of God. The origin of the distinction is in God, the distinction itself in the creature. As noted above, already Gregory of Nazianzen maintained that God is neither masculine nor feminine. *PG* 36, 140-146.

11. In Hindu mythology, the female is identified with the material element of creation, *Prakriti,* and the five important goddesses of the Hindu pantheon (Durga, Radha, Laksmi, Sarasvati, and Savitri), as well as all female beings, are regarded as parts or fractions of *Prakriti.* Cf. C.M. Brown, *God as Mother: A Feminine Theology in India* (Hartford, Vt.: Claude Stark & Co., 1974), 124, 142f. The Indo-European Aryans around 1500 B.C. took their male god, *Dyaus Pitar,* who became Zeus Pater and Jupiter with the Greeks and Romans, into northern India only to encounter a highly developed civilization of Harappa and Mohenjo-daro, whose chief divinity was apparently a female goddess. Thereafter the Aryans portrayed their "father-god" with his consort Prithivi, from whose union gods and men had their birth. The two correspond to heaven (the god) and earth (the goddess). Cf. Hamerton-Kelly, 22-23.

12. M. Hauke, *Women in the Priesthood?* 121-194, 216-196.

13. Irenaeus, *Adv. Haer.* I:23; Justin, *Apol.* I:26. The extent to which Irenaeus' genealogy of gnosticism may be the rhetorical style of the day is discussed by P. Perkins, "Irenaeus and the Gnostics," *VigChr* 30 (1976), 193-200.

14. An early second century gnostic Christian passage in the *Book of Elchasai* speaks of two enormous heavenly figures: "The male figure was the Son of God, but the female was called Holy Spirit." As found in Hippolytus, Ref. 9. 13. 1-3, trans. R. McL. Wilson in E. Hennecke, *New Testament Apocrypha* II (Philadelphia: Westminster, 1964), 746.

15. The gnostic influenced *Gospel of the Hebrews,* dating from the first half of the second century, places these words on the lips of Jesus: "Even so did my mother, the Holy Spirit, take me by one of my hairs and carry me away to the great mountain Tabor." Trans. P. Vielhauer in *New Testament Apocrypha* (Philadelphia: Westminster, 1964) 164. See also the apocryphal *Gospel of Philip,* in which the Spirit, not Mary, is the virgin- mother of Jesus (71:3-5, 16-19, NHL 143; 55:25-26, NHL 134 and Pagels, 63-64).

16. *Apocryphon of John* 2:9-14; in NHL 99.

17. Irenaeus, *Adv. Haer.* 1.5.4.; 1.29.4; 1.30.6; Hippolytus, *Ref. Om. Haer.,*

6:33; *Apocryphon of John* 13:5-14, NHL 105-106; *The Hypostasis of the Archons* 94:5-30, NHL 157-158.158.

18. P. Perkins, *The Gnostic Dialogue: The Early Church and the Crisis of Gnosticism* (New York: Paulist, 1980) 180-181.

19. K. Rudolph, *Gnosis: The Nature and History of Gnosticism,* tr. R.W. Wilson (San Francisco: Harper & Row, 1977), 61-65; P. Perkins, *The Gnostic Dialogue,* 166-171. See also Donald G. Bloesch, *The Battle for the Trinity* (Ann Arbor: Servant Publications, 1985), p. 48, referring to studies by Jonas and Laeuchli.

20. W. A. Visser't Hooft, *The Fatherhood of God in an Age of Emancipation* (Geneva: World Council of Churches, 1982), 132. The Valentinians, however, practiced marriage. Cf. E. Pagels, *The Gnostic Gospels* (New York: Random House, 1979), 174.

21. M. L. King, Jr., *The Strength to Love* (New York: Harper and Row, 1963); reprinted in *A Testament of Hope: The Essential Writings of Martin Luther King, Jr.* (San Francisco: Harper and Row, 1986), 516.

22. Elaine Pagels in her study of gnosticism (*The Gnostic Gospels* [New York: Random House, 1979] has raised the important question of the interrelation of religious metaphors and socio-political consequences. Thus: "when the orthodox insisted upon 'one God,' [against the gnostics] they simultaneously validated the system of governance in which the church is ruled by 'one bishop.' (40) Similarly, the male images of God prevailing among the orthodox had such political and social consequences as the barring of women from ecclesiastical office, whereas the female images admitted by the gnostics also allowed women to exercise such offices (though Pagels admits that the Marcionites, the Montanists and the Carpocratians, who admitted women to office, retained masculine images of God) (70-78). Pagels is enough of a scholar not to claim proof of a strict causal connection between religious metaphor and sociopolitical organization, and it is this proof in the gnostic controversy that one reviewer of her book finds wanting (D. P. Efryomson, TS 42 [1981] 136-138). This is a particularly delicate issue which should be resolved by strict validation rather than innuendo or assumption or mere synchronicity. Particularly, one should take account of the fact that groups using the same metaphor (e.g. a masculine image of God) drew differing consequences concerning admission of women to office; and also the fact that some of the gnostic literature is boldly anti-feminist (Pagels, 79-83).

23. J. H. Bernard, *The Odes of Solomon* (Cambridge U. Press, 1912), 67-68; J. H. Charlesworth, *The Odes of Solomon* (Oxford: Clarendon, 1973) 83.

24. See, for example, Hippolytus of Rome, *The Apostolic Tradition* 23, 2, where milk and honey are given to the baptized.

25. *Paidagogos* 1.6; trans. Pagels, 81.

26. Juliana of Norwich, *Revelations of Divine Love,* tr. M L. de Mastro (Garden City: Doubleday Image, 1977) 173. See also B. Pelphrey, *Christ Our Mother: Julian of Norwich* (Wilmington DL: Michael Glazier, 1989). It is of great significance, in the light of contemporary theological discussion, that Juliana does not develop her mother images of God in conflict with the title Father, but rather in the closest unity. She also uses the mother image of the church and of Mary, of whom she writes: "So our Lady is our mother, in whom we are all enclosed and born of her in Christ, for she who is mother of our saviour is mother of all who are saved in our saviour; [and then she proceeds to apply the maternal image to Christ] and our saviour is our true Mother, in whom we are endlessly born and out of whom we shall never come." *Julian of Norwich: Showings,* trans. E. Colledge and J. Walsh (New York: Paulist, 1978), ch. 57, 292. In the preface to this work, J. Leclercq comments: "What she develops is not the idea of femininity as opposed to or distinct from that of masculinity, but that of the motherhood of God as complement to that of his fatherhood. She does not introduce in her approach to God the vocabulary and the symbolism of sex . . . In no way does she wish to substitute the idea of the motherhood of God for that of his fatherhood. She wants to unite them." *Ibid.*, 11.

27. St. Anselm of Canterbury, *The Prayers and Meditations of St. Anselm,* tr. B. Ward (Penguin Classics, 1973), 153. For the same reason, even early tradition sometimes speaks of Christ as father. In *The Acts of Justin Martyr and His Companions,* recension B 4, from the middle of the second century, the martyr Hierax says: "Christ is our true father, and our faith in him is our mother" (*The Acts of the Christian Martyrs,* ed. Herbert Musurillo [Oxford: Clarendon, 1972] 50). Also from the same date the apocryphal *Second Letter to the Corinthians 2, 1, 4,* says of Christ: "He gave us light; as a father he called us sons" (*PG* 1,221). And Irenaeus writes: "The Word of God is the father of the human race" (*Against Heresies* 4, 31, 3 (SC 100, 793). Cf. K. McDonnell, "Communion Ecclesiology and Baptism in the Spirit: Tertullian and the Early Church," *TS* 49 (1988) 682.

28. See Caroline W. Bynum, *Jesus as Mother* (Berkeley: University of California, 1982); Y. M. G. Congar, *I Believe in the Holy Spirit* III (New York: Seabury, 1983) 156. See also B. Pelphrey, noted above.

29. I am grateful to my friend and colleague, Fr. Pat Gaffney, S.M.M., for this detail.

30. Leonardo Boff, *The Maternal Face of God: The Feminine and its Religious Expressions*, tr. R.R. Barr and J.W. Diercksmeier (San Francisco: Harper and Row, 1987), 3.

31. Ibid., 88.

32. *Insegnamenti di Giovanni Paolo I* (Libreria Editrice Vaticana 1979), 61; official English translation, *The Teachings of Pope John Paul I* (Libreria Editrice Vaticana), 7.

33. *Women in the Priesthood?* 229, n. 94.

34. William Oddie, *What Will Happen to God?* (San Francisco: Ignatius, 1988) 111-124, suggests that because metaphor is ordinarily used merely for comparisons on the horizontal level in our human experience and language, whereas here we are speaking of infinite transcendence and a participation in Jesus' own relation with the Father, the better word is *symbol*. Actually, he seems to come close to what Aquinas meant by analogy. In Thomistic terms, however, in describing how it is possible for a creature to share in the Trinitarian relationships, one would speak of a *relatio realis* in man and a *relatio rationis* in God—i.e., our participation in those relationships effects a real change in us without effecting a change in God.

35. Hence the difficulty I have with L. Boff's expression, "God the Mother engenders the humanity of the eternal son." *The Maternal Face of God,* 162.

36. D. A. Helminiak, "Doing Right by Women and the Trinity Too," *America* 160 (Feb. 11, 1989) 110-119.

37. See S. M. Schneiders, 50-67.

Part Two

MARY AND THE FEMININE FACE OF GOD

In the previous chapters we have seen how the Old Testament image of God, and even more so the image of God revealed by Jesus, overflowed the "Abba" metaphor, enriching it with feminine traits. In the New Testament, these feminine and maternal motifs are brought to fulfillment beyond expectations in an historical person, Mary, human reflection and visible sacrament of the feminine and maternal in God.

Our interest here is not archival; for in God's plan the past is for today. If the Holy Spirit inspired and directed the ever richer development of feminine motifs in the Old Testament, bringing them to convergence in Mary, then it was to actualize in us today their full meaning. Thus in the next chapter we ask whether and in what sense the the church's ongoing Marian experience is authored by the Holy Spirit, and then in the subsequent chapters we explore three major motifs that receive a Marian fulfillment in the New Testament: the Queen Mother, Virgin Daughter Zion, and Mother Zion. The Holy Spirit continues to use these motifs to bring the disciples of Jesus to conformity with him.

Chapter Three

THE HOLY SPIRIT: SOURCE OF THE MARIAN EXPERIENCE

Does the Spirit that cries, "Abba!" also cry, "Imma"? That familiar address to the child's mother, found alongside "Abba" in the Jewish Talmud, does not appear in the New Testament. It would be a mistake to conclude, however, that the Spirit knows no feminine face in its revealing and bonding role between God and his people.

Let me begin with a personal experience.

When the Peace Corps volunteer appeared at my door in Kathmandu, Nepal, where I lived and worked for six years, I had no idea of why she had come. But it didn't take long to find out. Seated in the bamboo cane chair facing me, she poured out the recent events in her spiritual journey, the latest of which was an article of mine she had read in *New Covenant* magazine. That article was really a selection from letters I had written to family and friends reflecting on my own experiences in a foreign land and how I felt the Lord's presence in the events of my life. But the reading had triggered something deep in this young woman's heart; she was desperately searching for God. Unchurched, she was not even asking to become a Catholic. She just wanted to be prayed over to receive the Holy Spirit.

Aware that the Lord does not always follow the logical steps now elaborated in the Rite of Christian Initiation of Adults, and remembering that in the Acts of the Apostles Ananias laid his hands on Saul before he was baptized (Acts 9:17-18) and that the Holy Spirit fell upon the gentile Cornelius and his company before they were baptized (Acts 10:44-48), I felt I should accede to her wishes. I laid my hands on her head and prayed that she be filled with the Holy Spirit. Her eyes filled with tears of joy, and she went to our chapel and prayed for a long time. Two years later I received her into the church, and celebrated her wedding to a Catholic Peace Corps worker who had also, in the meantime, experienced a powerful working of the Holy Spirit in his life.

Recently I received from her the following letter:

> My understanding is now beginning to be let in on the secrets that my heart has been attesting to since . . . well, since one Sunday afternoon three years ago when my burdened heart sought out an unknown priest in Kathmandu. How she led me to you I still can't imagine. Coming from a protestant background, I'm sure there were no rosaries being said for me. But she was there nonetheless. The

72

day after I first came to you I wrote a letter to a relative telling her that the Holy Spirit must be female in nature because I was certain I was receiving the love and protection of a woman. It has been only recently that I've begun to see how united Mary is with the Holy Spirit. And even though she only magnifies the Spirit, disappearing as he appears, something remains of her: a sweet companionship and the resonance of a perfect human joy.

I am still amazed at the fact that I asked you to teach us to pray the rosary. That was a miracle. Coming from my churchless background, I can't imagine how I even knew the word. But I remember the strong desire I had to learn about it. I was yearning for a deeper form of prayer. She must have known. Formal church prayers had in those early days no meaning for me. What prayer I did know was meditation, mostly through reading or writing. I knew the peace of mind and heart that came from the unraveling of an idea or feeling. The fruit was inward silence, and the revelation of a message of truth. But something was missing for me, a directness which seemed unobtainable through mind-led meditation. The rosary became for me a straighter path to contact with God because it is essentially a prayer of the heart. There is most definitely a place for the mind—those most profound of Christian mysteries. But the mind is led by the heart, whose leadership, at least for me, is more powerful. Perhaps you didn't know that as soon as you taught us the rosary, I began to pray five decades almost every day. It really filled a need in me. It seemed a perfect combination of simple praise and meditation.

I can't say that I knew Mary then. But I began to know of her through meditating on the mysteries, and more importantly through her presence in my life as I prayed to and with her. She answers all who call upon her name, even if we don't know the meaning of what we do. After my entrance into the church, she proceeded to intercede for her new daughter. She made sure that the Holy Spirit enlightened me to the wonders of my new life. This continues and I now find myself more Catholic than most Catholics I know! Any questions or concerns I had, I placed into her hands for prayer. In the beginning these had to do with the authority of the Pope, the power of the sacraments through the priests—basically with the supernatural reality of the church. My prayers were always answered, as one by one each point of confusion or doubt became solidified as faith.

When we first returned to the States, we attended Mass whenever possible as we traveled by car from San Francisco to Michigan. It was a joyful experience to be able to find this common faith in each little town we came to. Somewhere in Wyoming, a decision arose to begin praying a rosary every day for the conversion of my father, a wealthy, lonely man having no spiritual life at all. He had lived most of his adult life in the fast lane—lots of money, power and women. After two months of this commitment to prayer, Tim and I went to Washington D.C. to visit him. Visits in the past had caused me much anxiety—never knowing what kind of mood he'd be in. The previous visit had been three years before, after my having been in Africa for two years.

On the night of my arrival then he took me to dinner with some of his friends. They proceeded to drink champagne late into the night while I sat quietly watching. So I was a bit nervous about visiting him again. Upon arriving this time, though, I noticed a difference in him right away, a calmness. We sat quietly together outside that evening and he proceeded to ask me, most sincerely, about my spiritual life, how I had come to be converted and why I had chosen Catholicism. He asked me! Well, being a new Christian and having had little experience with answered prayer, I was quite amazed. Prayer really worked. All I could say was—O Mary, O Mary, O Mary! All of my efforts in the past to change this man seemed so superficial in light of what I was now witnessing. When the Spirit himself moves in a person, the change is so very natural and gentle. We shared a beautiful time together for the first time in many years, camping near the ocean and talking around our campfire for hours about God, Jesus, and the many questions he had.

After our return home, I was more fervent

than ever in praying the rosary for him, adding then to my prayer a commitment of physical sacrifice until his conversion would be fulfilled. A few months later, at Christmas time, we met again. When we walked in the door of my aunt's house, he gave me the biggest bear hug I'd ever had. I could feel his love just trembling within him. He told Tim and me over and over what an impact our life had had on him. (I didn't tell him that it was really Mary's petitions to the Holy Spirit that were working the miracle.) That evening he read from the Bible to the whole family. His mother was in tears. A Protestant, she had been praying for him for years. We spent a few very good days together before I had to leave. Our departure was a sad one because he was to leave a few months later for overseas, where he was hoping to open a small business and lead a simpler life away from the rat race of Washington. I didn't know when I would see him again. . .

Two nights ago, after I'd already begun writing this letter to you, I got a phone call from my father. He was full of joy. He'd been using his free time to read a book we'd given him, C.S. Lewis' *Mere Christianity*. He had read it twice and wanted to read everything C.S. Lewis had written. He was praying every day and said that he was really experiencing God's presence in his life, realizing how he'd led an evil life in the past but feeling full of hope now. He had faith that God would change him . . . And, as icing on my cake, he believes that he will soon become a Catholic! As I write this, for him it is Sunday morning. He has an appointment with a priest today. Hail Mary, full of grace, the Lord is with thee! This is nothing less than a miracle. It has been just less than a year since I've been asking Mary for her intercession for his soul.

It is easy to get the impression by reading of Mary's intercessory power that those who pray to her or with her, use her as a sort of magician. This is very far from the reality, and I say with all of my soul that my devotion to her isn't at all dependent upon these miracles. These are merely gifts that Jesus bestows on us through her. The real importance of devotion to Mary for me is that by virtue of the role given to her by God, she is the most direct path to Jesus. I believe that we are witnessing in our age the central role she plays in our redemption, not by any power of her own, but only because God chose her to be this channel. In my own life, as I mentioned before, she has been beside me as my Catholic faith deepened and as I desired to grow closer to Jesus in prayer. These moments of prayer are my most intimate witness of her presence. Time after time, usually while praying the rosary, my deepest questions are answered. During lent this year I had been asking to be led to a deeper devotion to and experience of Jesus in the Eucharist. In many special moments this prayer is being answered. I am always being brought closer to Christ, to the Holy Trinity and to her.

She has been beside me as mother, as friend and as Queen.

One day I was taking a walk in the woods, praying the rosary in a loud voice. I was feeling a heavy burden of prayer for some of my family members. Very clearly and directly enough to make me stop in my tracks, she said to me, "It is time now for you to take your prayers to Jesus in the tabernacle. I will be with you, pray with you, but you must now seek out time to spend with Jesus there." And that was that. I understood exactly what she meant and knew that this was what I really needed.

She is so much to me now that it is frustrating to attempt to write about it. Words cannot get at her pervasive role and the depth of her presence. She is in the depths of prayer and in the depths of each mystery of our faith. Take the fruit of any mystery which you need in your life and follow her . . . humility, faith, obedience—she will lead you oh, so directly into the center of the Trinity, where all mysteries are united.

I find the above testimony remarkable from several points of view: her experience of the feminine face of God through Mary and the Holy Spirit; her journey into the mystery of the church and its rich sacramental life, and ultimately into the life of the Trinity. The conversion of her father was a great grace received, she firmly believes, through Mary's intercession. But most importantly, the presence of Mary and the activity of the Holy Spirit has effected a transformation in her life.

If her experience were an isolated one, it would hardly merit reflection on its meaning for the church. But it is not. In the appendices I have gathered a number of other testimonies typical of Marian devotion, and it is easy to see in the experience of these Christians how the Holy Spirit uses the holy mother as a primary instrument in awakening persons to the mysteries of the faith and in deepening their union with the Lord.

Can the scriptures enlighten us on this apparent strategy of God? I believe they can. For that, we need to begin with an exploration of the role of the Holy Spirit in unwrapping the gift that Jesus is and the gifts that he has left us.

Memory and Revealer of Jesus

In his words to his disciples at the last supper, as reported in the fourth gospel, Jesus assigns a remarkable role to the Holy Spirit:

> The Advocate, the holy Spirit that the Father will send in my name—he will *teach* you everything and *remind* you of all that [I] told you (John 14:26).

Jesus has just said how aware he is that the many things he has told his disciples will remain mysteries to them, incomprehensible (14:25). John echoes this in another way when he says that Jesus did and said so many things that the whole world could not contain the books that would have to be written (21:25). He is referring, of course, not to the quantity of Jesus' deeds and words but to their unexplored depths. The Holy Spirit, sent in the *name* of Jesus—that is, in virtue of Jesus' self-gift on the cross and in replacement of him while he is with the Father— will teach the disciples everything they need to know. That teaching is, in part at least, a recalling of what Jesus did and said, but also a new insight into the past events. When the disciples after Jesus' resurrection remembered that he had spoken of raising up the temple in three days, they understood that he was referring to the temple of his body (2:21-22).

Paul describes this revealing role of the Holy Spirit in a slightly different way:

> "What eye has not seen, and ear has not heard,
>   and what has not entered the human heart,
> what God has prepared for those who love him,"
>   this God has *revealed* to us through the Spirit.
>
> For the Spirit scrutinizes everything, even the depths of God. Among human beings, who knows what pertains to a person except the spirit of the person that is within? Similarly, no one knows what pertains to God except the Spirit of God. We have not received the spirit of the world but the Spirit that is from God, so that we may *understand* the things freely given us by God (1 Cor 2:9-12).

Revelation is thus twofold. In its outer form it appears in all God's works *ad extra*. In creation, first of all, which is a true revelation of God (Rom 1:20). Then in the events of sacred history and in the words of Scripture that interpret those events, above all in the incarnation, life, death and resurrection of Jesus Christ and in the passing on of all of that in the ministry of the church. But that is only the outer form of revelation. Without the *inner* revelation by the Spirit, the outer revelation would do no more good than sunlight to a blind person. It is the Holy Spirit who effects the real encounter of the living person with the living word of God, who makes the outer revelation an inner experience. He is the foretaste of the world to come (Heb 6:4), the one who joins with our spirit to bear a common witness that we *are* indeed the children of God (Rom 8:15). The Holy Spirit is continually unwrapping for us the gifts we have received from God, so that we may enjoy them and use them for his glory.

Interpreter of the Treasures of Jesus

> "I have much more to tell you, but you cannot bear it now. But when he comes, the Spirit of truth, he will guide you to all truth. He will not speak on his own, but he will speak what he hears, and will declare to you the things that are coming. He will glorify me, because he will take from what is mine and declare it to you. Everything that the Father has is mine; for this reason I told you that he will take from what is mine and declare it to you" (John 16:12-15).

Similar to John 14:25-26 examined above, this text mentions first the *more* that has still not been *told* to the disciples. Again, this *more* means an interpretation, a deeper understanding and experience of what has already been given, for in the second sentence the Spirit of truth is described as a guide into all truth. It is not a new truth the Spirit creates; he explores the truth already given, who is Jesus himself ("I am . . . the truth," John 14:6). One who visits a cavern for the first time appreciates a guide to point out the marvels to be found there. The Spirit takes the role of Jesus himself, revealing only what he hears from Jesus and the Father. He is not an independent revealer.

"He will. . .declare to you the things that are coming." Does this mean he will inspire prophecy about future events? That is a possible meaning, and indeed among the New Testament prophets there was some forecasting of future events (cf. Acts 11:27-28; 21:10-11). But it is more likely that the word *anangellein*, translated "declare," has the meaning in which it is used in Daniel 2:2, 4, 7, where the prophet *declares the meaning* of the king's dream, that is, he interprets it. The dream is past; the interpretation is given later by someone other than the king. In this sense, the Paraclete will interpret for the disciples the ongoing events of their lives, presumably by linking them with Jesus' life and teaching. In this sense, just as the early Christians and the evangelists considered all of the Old Testament prophetic, so the life and teaching of Jesus is also prophetic for the future of the church. It is the role of the Holy Spirit to unfold the meaning of the future events as fulfilling the whole prophetic thrust of Jesus' life and teaching. An example: Jesus, just and innocent, was rejected and martyred. When the disciples experience the same treatment, they fulfill what was already somehow contained and forecast in Jesus' own passion, as well as his prophetic words that this would indeed happen (John 15:18-20).

The same richness of meaning underlies the use of *declare* in the next sentence: "He will take what is mine and declare it to you." Here, the sense is more than interpreting; to announce means also to *present*, as one would "announce" a visitor. Combining this with the previous texts we have considered, we are led to the conclusion that the Holy Spirit 1) Presents to the consciousness of the church the life giving mysteries of Jesus; 2) Interprets those mysteries; and 3) Gives the inner experience of those mysteries.

A movie projector shines a light through moving

celluloid frames onto a screen, thus bringing alive what otherwise would be unavailable to the audience. In a similar way, the Holy Spirit takes the scriptural accounts of Jesus' life, consigned to ink and paper, and brings them to life in the consciousness of the church. More, the Spirit invites the audience onto the stage, to participate in the "nowing" of the event.

What Belongs to Jesus

Jesus further says that what the Spirit presents and interprets is "what is mine." What are the "belongings of Jesus"? Surely first of all the Father, whom Jesus repeatedly calls his in a special way. Jesus is the revealer of the Father (John 1:18), but the Holy Spirit now continues the work of Jesus in revealing him. It is the Spirit that enables us to cry out, "Abba, Father!" and to know that we are God's children (Rom 8:15).

The Eucharist is certainly what belongs to Jesus. It is his flesh, his blood (John 6:55). The Holy Spirit activates an understanding of this sacramental mystery in the church, promotes Eucharistic devotion, and leads the church into an ever deeper appreciation of this gift.

Jesus' word is another of his "belongings" which the Spirit unfolds. Without the spirit, Jesus' words are dead to the listener: "It is the spirit that gives life; the flesh is of no avail. The words I have spoken to you are spirit and life" (John 6:63). The Holy Spirit guided the first preachers of the gospel and the writing evangelists in their interpretation and proclamation of the message of Jesus. And the commentaries of the fathers and doctors of the church, in an analogous if not identical way, were inspired by the Holy Spirit. The Spirit continues to unfold the meaning of the word for Christians today in prayer and in their daily living.

Jesus' disciples are one of his closest belongings—those disciples at the Last Supper whom he calls his "own," "the ones you have given me" (John 17:6), but also anyone who comes to him (John 6:37) and the sheep that are yet to be brought in: "I have other sheep that do not belong to this fold. These also I must lead" (John 10:16). This is the mystery of the church of Jesus; the Holy Spirit continues to reveal the mystery *of* the church *to* the church, from Paul's theology of the Body of Christ down to the Constitution on the Church by Vatican II.

And now we come to the goal of our inquiry. What belonged to Jesus was not only his Father, his word, his body and blood, his disciples, his church. Fully human being that he was, Jesus had a mother. In John's gospel, like the "disciple whom Jesus loved," she is nameless. Her identity comes only from her belonging to Jesus. She is "the mother of Jesus." Through her he took our flesh and became one of us. God did not use her and then cast her aside. He chose to make her a permanent, ongoing part of his revelation. The Holy Spirit who overshadowed her and conceived Jesus in her womb would continue to use her in his work of unfolding the mystery of Jesus, for she is a unique part of that treasury of Jesus which it is the Spirit's role to reveal.

The beginning of that revelation, its foundational stage, is the apostolic period, witnessed by the New Testament. In the gospels of Matthew, Luke and John particularly we see Mary as a key instrument of the Holy Spirit not merely in the enfleshing of the Word physically, as it were, but also in being the first, and in some ways the best, human resonance of the divine initiative, the first ripple

84

to the plunging of God into the waters of humanity, the good soil that first receives the seed, God's word, and feeds it with human love and life. In so doing, she becomes the Spirit's model for what he is about in every human soul and in the church at large. She is response and instrument.

Mary, Context for the Word

When in May 1988 I visited my brother Frank's home, the first thing that caught my eye was a large portrait of my deceased mother, which some artist had painted from the family's favorite photograph of her. I was stunned by how life-like the painting was, how vivid her blue eyes, the color of her cheeks, her silver hair. I was waiting for her to speak! What accounted for the brilliance of this portrait? It was not merely the work of the artist. It was the work of the one who framed the picture. The blue and mauve setting brought my mother to life!

A festive meal is twice as enjoyable if it is beautifully set out. A jewel calls for a gold burst, a tabernacle for a sanctuary, sex for a committed love. Setting gives meaning. It is the first interpreter of the object, the person or the event.

In the Father's plan, Mary is the context for Jesus. This is obvious in his conception, birth and childhood, for the child is always seen in its mother's arms or near her, dependent upon her. She receives the Word, enfleshes and nourishes the Word, presents him to the world. The Magi, forerunners of the gentiles, find "the child with Mary his mother" (Mt 2:11).

But Mary is more than a physical context for the Word made flesh. Her response, as Luke makes clear, is a model for all other responses. Whereas Zechariah hesitates, Mary is proclaimed blessed because she believed fully. Elizabeth cries out, "Blessed are you who believed that what was spoken to you by the Lord would be fulfilled" (Lk 1:45). And Jesus later answers the woman who blesses his mother: "Rather, blessed are those who hear the word of God and observe it" (Lk 11:28).

I remember once seeing a televised talk by Fr. John Powell, S.J. It was a beautiful talk, delivered flawlessly without notes. But the camera spent at least one third of the time on the faces of the audience. Not only did such a technique provide variety, but the rapt faces of the audience, some of them obviously his close friends, interpreted for the television audience what Father Powell was saying. A smile, a confirming nod, a moment of shared anguish—these were schooling the unseen listeners in understanding and response to the speaker and his message.

The New Testament provides a similar echo of Jesus' life and words in those who surround him—though it is by far more courageous in detailing negative as well as positive responses, the negative ones functioning to highlight all the more the positive ones. Among the positive ones, for Luke at least, Mary, the Mother of Jesus, is outstanding. She is the Spirit-inspired context for the Word, who is her own Son. And in so doing she schools response for the disciples of all ages.

Mary's contextual function has been particularly marked in the tradition of the eastern churches, where iconography has given a special place to the mother and child. But Christian art of all cultures has revelled in setting Jesus in the context of Mary. Just as in the Old Testament, the psalms are an inspired response to the word of God, so in the new dispensation, Mary is the spirit-filled response to God's initiative, and thus she becomes part of the revelation process itself, both in the New Testament and in the ongoing assimilation of the gospel by the church. If the Gospel is the playing out in history of God's victory through Jesus, then Mary is God's first cheerleader.

Mary as Channel

Mary as model-of-response blends into Mary as channel of the Holy Spirit in effecting God's work in the new creation. Abraham's "yes" was the first moment of his becoming the instrument of God's saving purpose. Mary's "yes" not only released the power of the Holy Spirit to enflesh the Word through her, but the Incarnation enabled by her response also becomes the pattern for the spiritual rebirth of others.

In the Scriptural evidence we are about to examine, these two themes of response and fruitful instrumentality will be interwoven.

Chapter Four

THE QUEEN MOTHER

For all its patriarchalism, the Old Testament gives a surprising amount of attention to women. Three books are dedicated to women heroines: Ruth, Judith and Esther. And in the great sagas we encounter the key roles of Sarah, Rebecca, Rachel, Miriam, the prophetess Deborah, Jael who slew Sisera the Canaanite general, the prophetess Hulda—and the list could go on. But the most significant forerunner of the New Testament Mary, the motif that gives us the greatest understanding of Mary's role in God's revelation, is the Old Testament role of the Queen Mother.

Origins

During the desert years and the first years of occupation of the promised land, Israel had no king but Yahweh, the covenant God of Sinai. Moses had not been a king, only the intermediary between the invisible God-king and his people. And during the early years of the conquest, leadership rested in charismatic leaders, "Judges" as they were called, folk heroes, men or women, who rallied the scattered tribes and led them against their enemies. But it was not long till the people, faced with the Philistine menace, begged the priest-prophet Samuel to anoint a king. Samuel was opposed to the idea, pointing out that the Lord was their only king and that, for whatever boon they might introduce, kings would bring oppression. But the will of the people prevailed, and thus with the anointing of Saul human royalty entered the history of Israel.

After Saul, the kingship became hereditary with David. At least that tradition was maintained in Judah after the split of the kingdoms, while the northern kingdom was rent by dynastic wars and succession based on intrigue. But in the southern kingdom, legitimacy of claims to the throne was judged by fidelity to Nathan's prophecy that David's house would last forever (2 Sam 7:16).

The early kings fashioned their court on the pattern of other kings, with a harem of many wives. Usually one of the women was the king's favorite, but none of them, in the kingdom of Judah, was ever queen. Yet there was the equivalent of the queen in what was called the *Gebira*, the "Great Lady." She was not the king's wife, but his mother. She was given special honor, and because she alone of all the previous king's wives, gave birth to the successor, she is habitually mentioned in the succession lists of the kings of Judah.[1] In striking contrast, the author of the book of Kings, shows no interest in the mothers of the northern kings of Israel.[2]

The *Gebira*, whom hereafter we shall call the queen mother, shared the throne with her son. When Jeremiah predicts exile, he says, "Say to the king and to the queen mother: come down from your throne; From your heads fall your magnificent crowns" (Jer 13:18). The fulfillment of this prophecy is described in 2 Kgs 24:12, 15: "Then Jehoiachin, king of Judah, together with his mother, his ministers, officers and functionaries, surrendered to the king of Babylon . . . He deported Jehoiachin to Babylon, and also led captive from Jerusalem to Babylon the king's *mother* and wives, his functionaries, and the chief men of the land." The book of Jeremiah alludes to this event involving king and queen mother again in Jer 29:2.

A remarkable passage is 1 Kgs 2:19, in which Bathsheba, the queen mother, enters the presence her son, King Solomon, on a mission of intercession:

> Then Bathsheba went to King Solomon to speak to him for Adonijah, and the king stood up to meet her and paid her homage. Then he sat down upon his throne, and a throne was provided for the king's mother, who sat at his right.

This passage shows not only that the queen mother occupied a throne at the right side of her son, not only that she had the right to intervene in the affairs of state, but that the King, who was accustomed to receive the bowing homage of his wives (1 Kgs 1:16), would rise from his throne to bow in homage to his queen mother.

During one particularly dark period of Judah's history, Athaliah, queen mother of the slain King Ahaziah, ruled in his stead for six years (1 Kgs 11:1-3). A woman became queen mother the moment her son became king, and she retained the title until her death, even if a new king came to the throne. Such was the case of Maacah, who was queen mother during the reign of her son Abijam and her grandson Asa (1 Kgs 15:2, 10).

The queen mother's power was always subordinate to that of the king, but she had great moral influence. She was an honored counselor, at times representing certain particular political interests of the people to the king. Monarchy in Judah was, after all, never absolute. The king's counselors were prophets and wise men and priests and—as senior counselor—the king's mother. In an astounding passage in Proverbs 31:1-9, the queen mother instructs the king on how to rule the kingdom—to avoid obsession with his harem and excessive drinking and to take care of the poor who are without recourse. Formulas of instruction for kings such as this one are well known from the documents of the Near East, but only in this text of Proverbs is the instruction given to the king *by his mother.*[3]

The reasons for this exceptional role were not merely her physical closeness to the king but the theological foundations of the Davidic dynasty going back to the prophecy of Nathan (2 Sam 7:11-16). On the throne the queen mother represented the king's continuity with the past, the visible affirmation of God's ongoing plan for his people, the channel through which the Lord's dynastic promise to David was fulfilled. Mother that she was, she was a living reminder of the present king's father by whose grace he ruled. She was also a symbol of election, for it was not automatic that succession would pass to the former king's eldest surviving son. When David chose Solomon, he passed over the elder Adonijah (1 Kgs 1:11-40). This choice was seen even by Adonijah as the Lord's election of Solomon (1 Kgs 2:15), a view reaffirmed in the tradition (1 Chron 28:5).

Later, when the Judean kings proved such miserable ministers of God's plans for his people, the prophets resolved their disappointment by proclaiming that the promises made to the incumbent king would be transferred to the future king. Since in some cases this future king had not even been born, the spotlight fell upon the woman who would carry the future of Israel in her womb—the next queen mother. The most outstanding example of this is the Immanuel prophecy of Isaiah given to King Ahaz.

Briefly, the background is this. During the reign of Ahaz, who ruled Judah from 735 to 715 B.C., King Rezin of Aram and King Pekah of Israel, the northern kingdom, thought they had a chance to wrest themselves free of Assyrian domination, and they asked Ahaz to join them in this effort. When Ahaz refused, they sought to force his compliance by advancing their armies onto Jerusalem in the hope of deposing Ahaz and setting their own puppet king on the throne. This would, of course, break the Davidic line and annul the divine promise. Ahaz, frightened by this unexpected enmity from the north, feverishly sought to shore up the city's defenses. He was hardly a sincere Yahwist, however, for he had immolated his own son by fire in sacrifice to the pagan god Moloch, thus showing himself indifferent to the Lord's promise to his dynasty. Isaiah met Ahaz as he was supervising the waterworks and advised him to put his faith in Yahweh rather than in the pagan gods: "Unless your faith is firm, you shall not be firm" (Is 7:9).

That initiative having fallen on deaf ears, Isaiah again approached Ahaz, telling him that he should ask for a sign from the Lord—any kind of sign at all. Ahaz hypocritically replied that he would not dare tempt God by demanding a sign. To which Isaiah retorted:

> Listen, O house of David! Is it not enough for you to weary men, must you also weary my God? Therefore the Lord himself will give you this sign: the virgin shall be with child, and bear a son, and shall name him Immanuel (Is 7:13).

Isaiah addresses Ahaz as "house of David" because that is precisely what is at stake, the dynastic succession promised to David through the prophecy of Nathan. Since Ahaz has refused to show even enough faith to ask for a sign, the Lord will give one of his own choosing. Though translated "virgin" here, the Hebrew *almah* means a young woman of marriageable age, and in the historical context most scholars think it refers to Abi (or Abijah), the young bride of Ahaz, who will bear the successor to Ahaz, the future king Hezekiah. Ahaz' role in begetting his successor is, because of his lack of faith in the divine promise, passed over in favor of the instrumentality of the future queen mother. She, not Ahaz, will name the child Immanuel, the title meaning "God-with-us," because, despite the difficulties he may encounter, his reign will manifest the presence of the Lord in fufillment of the covenant promises.

Two things are remarkable about this prophecy: (1) Messianism is no longer a program for the incumbent king but for a future king. (2) Because it is a future king that is envisioned and the present king has been an unworthy transmitter of the promise, it is the *mother* of the future king who passes on the promise.

It is not surprising, then, that a contemporary of Isaiah, Micah of Moresheth, should foretell the Messiah in terms of his mother:

But you, Bethlehem-Ephrathah
    too small to be among the clans of Judah,
From you shall come forth for one
    one who is to be ruler in Israel;
Whose origin is from of old,
    from ancient times.
(Therefore the LORD will give them up, until the
    time when *she who is to give birth has borne,*
And the rest of his brethren shall return
    to the children of Israel.)
He shall stand firm and shepherd his flock
    by the strength of the LORD,
    in the majestic name of the LORD his God;
And they shall remain, for now his greatness
    shall reach to the ends of the earth;
    he shall be peace (Micah 5:1-4).

In the New Testament

We are now in a position to appreciate the role of Mary, mother of the eschatological Messiah. In the annunciation to Mary as portrayed by Luke, we read:

> "Behold, you will conceive in your womb and bear a son, and you shall name him Jesus. He will be great and will be called Son of the Most High, and the Lord God will give him the throne of David his father, and he will rule over the house of Jacob forever, and of his kingdom there will be no end."
> (Luke 1:31-33)

Given the role of the mother of the Messiah, which we have seen in the Old Testament passages above, it would be surprising if there were *not* some mention of the mother of Jesus in the Jewish portrayal of Jesus-Messiah. In fact, Luke alludes to the Immanuel prophecy of Isaiah 7:14

in the words, "*you* shall name him. . ." and to the prophecy of Nathan to David promising him an everlasting dynasty. The difference is that there will be no kings *after* Jesus, for he will himself rule forever. Though it is only implied in the text, any Jew hearing this would understand that Mary is here being given the vocation of queen mother.

There is, however, a significant advance in Luke over the motifs associated with the queen mother in the Old Testament. The texts of Isaiah and Micah, like those of the succession lists, say nothing about the conscious assent or response of the woman to her vocation to mother the future king. The most that we see in Isaiah is the use of King Ahaz as a counterexample of faith response. But Luke chooses to describe the encounter of the divine messenger with Mary in detail, and he focuses on her free, obedient faith response as a key element in the drama of salvation. She thus becomes the model of response for each disciple and for the church: "Blessed are you who believed. . ." (Lk 1:45). In contrast to doubting Zechariah, Mary accepts fully and faithfully her call, echoing Abraham's faith response which inaugurated the people of God. In the Old Testament the woman had no way of knowing that she was to be queen mother when she conceived the child who would be chosen king. In the New Testament, the Lord brings Mary into the picture at the very beginning, asking her consent to mother the eschatological Messiah-King.

There is still another way in which Mary is fulfillment of the queen mother beyond expectations. Her conception of Jesus is virginal. That means that her role as mother of the Messiah-King does not point to her Son's immediate predecessor on the throne of David, as did the queen mothers of the Old Testament. On the contrary, she points to the Father, the divine king who has sent his Son to take the vacant throne of David.

Though Matthew does not use the term queen mother, he clearly highlights Mary's role in the birth of the Messiah in several ways: (1) In an anticipatory way, by naming four women in the genealogy whose manner of conception was unusual; (2) By showing that at the last link the male descendence is bypassed through Mary's virginal conception of Jesus; (3) By explicitly quoting Isaiah 7:14 and Micah 5:1; (4) By noting that the Magi see the child "with Mary his mother" (Mt 2:11).

Matthew makes it very clear that the infant is king, Israel's messiah, son of David (1:1, 20; 2:2, 6, 11). Clearly, Mary is the Gebirah, the queen mother.

The transfer of the Old Testament motifs of the queen mother to Mary has not been sufficiently exploited in many books on Mary. The queen mother was honored by her son; she was a recognized power at the court; she often interceded with the king for favors; and she had a throne next to his.

This last point is worth examining more closely. During his earthly life, Jesus for the most part concealed his messiahship. He was never enthroned, and he sedulously avoided an attempt to make him king (John 6:15). But Peter in Acts proclaims that God, by raising Jesus from the dead, has enthroned and proclaimed him as the Messiah, quoting the Old Testament royal enthronement psalm 110:

> God has raised this Jesus; of this we are all witnesses. Exalted at the right hand of God [an Old Testament term for the enthronement of the king

in the palace at the right hand of the temple], he received the promise of the holy Spirit from the Father . . . For David did not go up into heaven, but he himself said: The Lord said to my Lord, "Sit at my right hand until I make your enemies your footstool." Therefore let the whole house of Israel know for certain that God has made him both Lord and Messiah, this Jesus whom you crucified (Acts 2:32-36).

Mary's assumption and coronation as queen of heaven is nowhere recorded in the New Testament. However, that the church should come to this belief appears a most logical consequence of meditating on what it meant in biblical terms for God to have chosen her as mother of the King who was enthroned in glory by resurrection from the dead. Or, if I may modify a poem by Fr. Finn, changing "home" to "throne," the logic of Catholic faith would be this:

> Nor Bethlehem nor Nazareth
> Apart from Mary's care
> Nor heaven itself a throne for him
> Were not his mother there.

We may conclude then, that while the feminine does not appear titularly within the Trinity, the image of woman does appear richly in the work of salvation, viewed as we have here under the limited perspective of the queen mother. To the Old Testament's intimate association of the queen mother with the coming Messiah, implying a reigning with him, Luke further portrayed the eschatological queen mother, Mary, as a model of faith response as well, thus making her not only the exalted throne-companion of her son but a fellow pilgrim for the faith community of Jesus' disciples. In the Judeo-

Christian tradition, however, the female companion of the divine king is not consort (as, for example Parvati is to Shiva) but mother. This combined image of king and queen mother, which reaches back to the earliest days of Israelite kingship, reaches forward in the church in its icons and images of mother and child, in the scene of Mary at the foot of the cross, Jesus' earthly throne, and in the apotheotic scenes of Mary crowned with her Son as queen of heaven and earth.[4]

The Queen Mother in our Christian Life

If the function of the Holy Spirit in the Christian life is what we described it to be in the previous chapter, then Mary as Queen Mother is part of the treasures of Jesus which the Spirit activates in the heart of the Christian and the heart of the Church, using that image to promote the kingdom, growth in faith, hope and love, the unity of the church and ultimately the glory of the Trinity. What stands out in the Queen Mother image is clearly her exaltedness, her closeness to her all powerful Son, her power of intercession. We know, of course, that this position of privilege is proportionate to the humble faith by which she declared herself the handmaid of the Lord, thus demonstrating the gospel principle that the lowly will be exalted, as she indeed sang in her Magnificat. We know too that Mary has nothing of her own that has not been given to her, and that her queenship is totally oriented to glorifying her Son, the king. Nevertheless, the biblical motif of the queen mother, brought to its consummation and fulfillment in Mary, will lead the Christian who claims to have Jesus enthroned in his or her heart to enthrone the mother of the king beside him.

The queen mother motif thus gives biblical validation

to those Christian experiences which venerate Mary under the aspects of queen and powerful intercessor. And since in addition the New Testament exploits Mary's response to her call in a way unanticipated in the Old Testament queen mothers, she is also the Holy Spirit's way of schooling response to God's call in our lives.

NOTES

1. Naamah, mother of King Rehoboam (1 Kgs 14:21); Maacah, mother of Abijam (1 Kgs 15:2); Azubah, mother of Jehoshahpat (l Kgs 22:42); Athaliah, mother of Ahaziah (2 Kgs 8:26); Zibiah, mother of Joash (1 Kgs 12:2); Jehoaddin, mother of Amaziah (2 Kgs 14:2); Jecholiah, mother of Azariah (2 Kgs 15:2); Jerusha, mother of Jothan (2 Kgs 15:33); Abi, mother of Hezekiah (2 Kgs 18:2); Hephzibah, mother of Manasseh (2 Kgs 21:1); Meshullemeth, mother of Amon (2 Kgs 21:19); Jedidah, mother of Josiah (2 Kgs 22:2); Hamutal, mother of Jehoahaz (2 Kgs 23:31); Zebidah, mother of Jehoia*kim* (2 Kgs 23:36); Nehushta, mother of Jehoia*chin* (2 Kgs 24:8); Hamutal, mother of Zedekiah (2 Kgs 24:18). The only exceptions are Asa, whose grandmother Maacah is mentioned as the Gebira, since she was still living (1 Kgs 15:10) and retained her title until death; Jehoram and Ahaz, both of whom are given very negative ratings by the author of the book of Kings.

2. Jezebel is the only apparent exception. She is mentioned as the *gebira* in 2 Kings 10:13, but otherwise there is no concern for dynastic succession in the northern kingdom through the queen mother.

3. N. A. Andreasen, "The Role of the Queen Mother in Israelite Society," *CBQ* 45 (1983) 192.

4. For further study of the Old Testament motif of the queen mother as a paradigm for understanding Mary see the references given by Andeasen, 194: G. F. Kirwim, *The Nature of the Queenship of Mary* (Washington: Catholic University of America dissertation, 1973); B. M. Nolan, *The Royal Son of God* (Göttingen: Vandenhoeck & Ruprecht, 1979) 41-43; H. Cazelles, "La mére du Roi-Messie dans l'Ancien Testament," *Acta congressus mariologici-mariani in civitate Lourdes anno 1958 celebrati: Maria et Ecclesia* 5 (1959) 48-56.

Chapter Five

VIRGIN DAUGHTER ZION

There is another biblical motif that converges on Mary in the New Testament: daughter Zion. Among the Semites, a large city, particularly a capital city, was often portrayed as mother and the outlying villages under her protection as daughters. Eventually the word "daughter" came to be applied to the major city itself, which, in the case of Jerusalem, capital of the Davidic kingdom, also became metonymy for the entire people. We have already noted in Chapter 2 how frequently this image occurs in the Lamentations over fallen Jerusalem. The term, though, had already been used by the prophets. Not only was it an image that crystallized the people's conscious-ness of their unity; it lent itself beautifully to the cove-nant theology which was at the heart of Israel's identity as a nation. And it merged with that other feminine image of covenant response, the spouse.

103

Spouse

It was Hosea who first introduced the spousal imagery in his plea to Israel to return to its covenant God and in his promise that the Lord would one day restore its pristine fidelity:

> On that day, says the LORD,
> She shall call me "My husband,"
> and never again "My baal" (Hos 2:18).

> I will espouse you to me forever:
> I will espouse you in right and in justice,
> in love and in mercy;
> I will espouse you in fidelity,
> and you shall know the LORD (Hos 2:21-22).

Jeremiah picked up Hosea's imagery and used it poignantly:

> I remember the devotion of your youth,
> how you loved me as a bride,
> Following me in the desert,
> in a land unsown (Jer 2:2).
> "...you who are the bridegroom of my youth"
> (Jer 3:4).

This image is richly exploited in the New Testament. Jesus is the bridegroom, his people the bride (Mk 2:19-20; John 3:29), and Christian marriage is to be modeled on this union (Eph 5:21-33). The church is the Jerusalem from above (Gal 4:26), and this new Jerusalem is spouse:

> I also saw the holy city, a new Jerusalem, coming down out of heaven from God, prepared as a bride adorned for her husband. I heard a loud voice from the throne saying, "Behold, God's dwelling is with the human race. He will dwell with them and they

will be his people and God himself will always be with them [as their God]. (Rev 21:2-3)

Daughter Zion, Virgin

The prophets often call Jerusalem or the people not merely "daughter Zion" but "virgin." To the king of Assyria threatening Jerusalem, the prophet taunts:

> She despises you, laughs you to scorn,
>   the virgin daughter Zion;
> Behind you she wags her head,
>   daughter Jerusalem (Is 37:22).

What does the note of virginity add to daughter Zion? We can guess it from the following text of Jeremiah:

> Truly horrible things has virgin Israel done! . . . yet my people have forgotten me: they burn incense to a thing that does not exist (Jer 18:13).

Israel's virginity, then, is her call to maintain herself pure of idolatrous deviations in her single-hearted devotion to Yahweh, her spouse. Her covenant call is the basis for Jeremiah's plea: "Turn back, O virgin Israel . . . How long will you continue to stray, rebellious daughter?" (Jer 31:21-22). Restoration of her covenant purity is part of her promised future: "Again I will restore you, and you shall be rebuilt, O virgin Israel" (Jer 31:4). It is clear, then, that Zion's virginity is a virginity of *faith* and *fidelity*. And that is precisely the sense in which Paul uses it in 2 Cor 11:2:

> . . . I betrothed you to one husband to present you as a chaste virgin to Christ.

105

Mary as Virgin Daughter Zion

A number of scholars, both Catholic and Protestant, have found in Luke's account of the annunciation to Mary a fulfillment of the Old Testament motif of Jerusalem as Daughter Zion. Stressing the Jewish background to the text, they note that the angel's first word to Mary is not the usual Jewish "Peace" but the Greek *chaire*, which translates the Hebrew "Rejoice" and evokes those Old Testament texts where the prophet announces salvation to daughter Zion:

> Rejoice heartily, O daughter Zion, shout for joy, O daughter Jerusalem! See, your king shall come to you; a just savior is he,...(Zech 9:9).

Note the words *rejoice, king,* and *savior,* all of which recur in the annunciation to Mary—Mary is told to rejoice, because she will bear a son who will be Savior (the name "Jesus") and king.

Even more specific a textual precedent is Zephaniah 3:14-18. It is a text addressed to the people under the title daughter Zion. I have used my own translations to bring out the parallels more literally. Note the parallels with the annunciation to Mary:

Zephaniah 3:14-18	Luke 1:28-33
Rejoice, O daughter Zion! sing joyfully, O Israel!	28: *Rejoice,* O favored one!
Be glad and exult with all your heart, O daughter Jerusalem...	
The King of Israel, *the Lord,* is *in your midst* . . .	*The Lord* is *with you*

106

Fear not, O Zion,	*Fear not,* Mary . . . you
be not discouraged!	shall conceive *in your*
The Lord, your God,	*womb* and name him
is in your midst,	*"Lord-Savior."*
a mighty *savior.*	

There are two points that need to be explained in the above comparison of texts. (1) The Jewish word for Jesus is *Yeshuah*, which means "the Lord saves" or "Lord is Savior." (2) In Hebrew the word *beqirbek* can mean "in your midst" when it is used of a city (as in Zephaniah's text), but the same word when used of a woman can mean "in your womb" (Gen 25:22). Luke would then understand the Zephaniah prophecy about the Lord coming into the *midst* of his people as fulfilled by the Lord-Savior coming into the womb of Mary. Thus Luke would see Mary as daughter Zion, no longer a personification but a person.

The above exegesis—that is, whether Luke really had in mind the text of Zephaniah—has been challenged by a number of scholars. "Rejoice" (the same Greek greeting *chaire* or *chairete*) is used as a normal greeting in Matthew 26:49 and 27:29. And was Luke, accustomed to using the Greek Old Testament, aware of the polyvalent meaning of the Hebrew *beqirbek*?

It is in the Magnificat that Mary's embodiment of the collectivity of Israel becomes clearest. The prophets had spoken of the future remnant of the people as "daughter Zion" or "daughter Jerusalem" (Micah 4:6-8). "my spirit rejoices in God my savior" (Lk 1:47) echoes the hymn in Hab 3:18: "I will rejoice in the Lord, and exult in my saving God." "All generations will call me blessed" (Lk 1:48) echoes "All nations will call you blessed" said of the land of Israel in Mal 3:12. In the noncanonical IV

Esdras 9:45, Zion says, "God has heard his servant; he has looked on my lowliness . . . and given me a son." "The Mighty One has done great things for me" (Lk 1:49) echoes ". . . your God has done for you those great . . . things" said of Israel (Deut 10:21). Finally, the reference to Abraham at the end of the Magnificat raises the question not only of the patriarch's role embodying all his descendants but Mary's similar role of corporate personality. To Mary as to Abraham concerning the future birth of the child the angel said "Nothing is impossible with God" (Lk 1:37; Gen 18:14). Like Abraham, she is told to "fear not" (Lk 1:30; Gen 15:2); like him, she has "found favor" with God (Lk 1:30; Gen 18:3).

There can be no doubt that for Luke Mary is not only the physical mother of Jesus. She is the model of response to the word. Proclaimed blessed because she believed (1:45), she "kept all these things, pondering them in her heart" (2:19, 51). Along with the "brothers of Jesus," she hears and acts on the word and is thus the good soil that bears fruit in messianic abundance (8:15, 21). Again in 11:27-28 Jesus proclaims her blessed because she listens to the word of God and keeps it. Finally, after the ascension of Jesus she is with the community gathered in prayer and awaiting the coming of the Spirit (Acts 1:14). Her song of praise is not only a personal one but voices the rejoicing of daughter Zion at the fulfillment of the promises made of old (1:46-55). Thus there was ample basis for the title given to Mary by the Second Vatican Council in its Constitution on the Church, where she is called "the exalted Daughter Zion" (*Lumen Gentium,* #55).

That she is virgin is a further fulfillment of those texts which depict Jerusalem as *virgin*. Mary's virginity is physical but more importantly it is a virginity of faith, as her perfect response indicates. She thus not only fulfills the Old Testament promise but models the virginity of the heart, the virginity of faith, which is that of the church.

Cana: The Messianic Wedding Feast

In John's book of signs, the wedding at Cana, the "first of Jesus' signs" (Jn 2:11), is perhaps the richest in symbolism. Like the six other signs which form John's structure of Jesus' public life, this sign is not just a miracle. It is a profound symbolic teaching on the meaning of Jesus' entire life and particularly his passion, death, and resurrection, the "hour" which is anticipated here (2:4). Like spokes leading to the hub of a wheel, each sign Jesus works points to the cross-resurrection. That event, we are told here, will celebrate the wedding of the Lord with his people, as foretold by Hosea (2:21-22); there Jesus will pour out the new wine of the Messianic wedding feast.

Cana is a foretaste and a symbol of what is to come. Strangely, though it is a wedding feast, the bride and groom nowhere appear in the story. The two major figures are Jesus and Mary. Now we know that in John's imagery Jesus is the bridegroom (3:29). Does Mary function here as the real bride of the Messianic feast?

There are some indications that this is so. Remembering that the image of spouse and/or virgin-daughter is a metaphor for the people's covenant relationship with the Lord, Mary's words to the servants, "Do whatever he tells you" (RSV) echo the obedient response given by the people in the desert when the covenant was first established: "Everything the LORD has said, we will do" (Ex 19:8). Furthermore, the title "Woman," which Jesus gives to

109

Mary is not the normal address given by a Jewish son to his mother. A Jew could use it, however, of another woman, and it was the common title by which a Jew would address his wife. Thus a number of scholars see the Cana wedding feast as a symbolic teaching of Jesus' own marriage to the new messianic people. But since it is difficult to visualize how he could espouse a collectivity, Mary provides the concrete personification here.

One might object that Mary's real role as mother of Jesus confuses the symbolism here—how can a woman be mother and spouse at the same time? Aside from the fact that biblical authors have fewer qualms about mixing figures of speech than modern grammarians do (see for example in the Pauline literature, the "building grows" and the "body is built up"), we might recall from the previous chapter how the mother of the King in Judah shared the throne with him, a role which in the northern kingdom and among other sovereigns, was that of the king's wife.

To unwrap all the symbolism contained in the Cana story would go beyond our purpose here. Suffice it to say that Mary appears in the story as the educator to covenant response: "Do whatever he tells you." Thus the motif of Daughter Zion, the virgin spouse, personalized in Mary, appears in the New Testament as a powerful tool of the Holy Spirit to deepen the early church's understanding of her own identity. The Holy Spirit continues to use her in this role to nurture the church to an appreciation of herself as mystery, as a mystical communion of all its members with Christ the spouse. That communion also suggests a passionate, devoted, faithful love on the part of both Christ and the church, the ground and the call for all those mystics who have spoken of the Christian life as a spousal relationship with Christ. And, following Ephesians 5, Christian married couples may look to this mystery of the church, embodied in Mary, as the inspiration of their own married love.

God cannot of himself embody human response to God. But Mary can—and does. In this aspect, Mary's spousal relationship shows human response rather than God's feminine face. But in the New Testament, particularly in Luke and John, the human response makes possible in time and history God's own engendering action. To this mystery we now turn.

Chapter Six

"BEHOLD YOUR MOTHER"

The final and most profound motif that we encounter, and it is with the fourth evangelist, is Mary as spiritual mother, a development and actualization of the Old Testament motif of Mother Zion. The key text is a brief one:

> Standing by the cross of Jesus were his mother and his mother's sister, Mary the wife of Clopas, and Mary of Magdala. When Jesus saw his mother and the disciple there whom he loved, he said to his mother, "Woman, behold your son." Then he said to the disciple, "Behold your mother." And from that hour the disciple took her into his home (John 19:25-27).

Jesus' last gesture from the cross has been variously interpreted in the Christian tradition. For some, it is simply a manifestation of Jesus' concern that his mother

113

be cared for after his death. This assumes, of course, that Joseph is no longer on the scene or at least that he is not capable of providing for her. The beloved disciple would take the place not only of Joseph, but of Jesus himself in fulfilling this responsibility toward Mary.

This level of meaning is certainly the most obvious. But if it is only that, then it would stand in strange isolation among the other scenes of Jesus' hour, each of which has also a symbolic meaning. The crucifixion with the inscription which Pilate placed on the cross had a deep and universal symbolism (19:17-22). In the seamless tunic the evangelist probably sees a symbol of Jesus' priesthood (19:23). In the dividing of the garments there is an explicit scripture fulfillment (19:24). When Jesus dies and "hands over the spirit" (19:20), the evangelist sees an anticipation of Jesus' giving the Spirit to the church, and the water and the blood flowing from Jesus' side symbolize not only the gift of the Spirit but probably the sacraments of baptism and eucharist as well (19:24).[1] So we can assume that beyond the factual event of confiding Mary to the beloved disciple, the evangelist sees a fulfillment of some divinely prepared promise. This is confirmed by what is immediately added in verse 28: "After this, aware that everything was now finished. . ." which indicates that he has just done a solemn final act which was "in his script," i.e., somehow foretold by the scriptures.

Moreover, there is another important fact: upon examination, we discover that the scene between Jesus and his mother is the central episode in a series arranged symmetrically, beginning with Jesus' crucifixion and ending with his burial. This scene is the keystone of a carefully constructed arch, which Raymond Brown has noted

114

and on which I have slightly expanded,[2] as is shown in the following diagram:

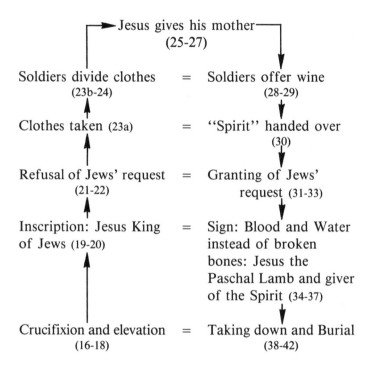

What then is the symbolism and teaching of this central scene? We may begin by asking who or what is symbolized by the principal characters and then go on to look at what actually takes place.

The Disciple

The beloved disciple plays a major role in John's gospel. He is the one who leans on Jesus' breast at the last supper (13:23). He is the one whose love for the Lord—and not simply his youth—gives him greater speed than Peter in running to the tomb (20:1-10). And, though he respects Peter as his elder by not entering the tomb before him, when the beloved disciple sees the wrappings and the head cloth, he believes (20:8), that is, he has an intuition of faith in Jesus' resurrection before anyone else. He is unique in that, of all the disciples, he believes *before* seeing the risen Lord, on the basis of a sign, the first to experience the blessing of believing without having to see (20:29). It is also the beloved disciple who will first recognize Jesus appearing to the disciples on the shore of Tiberias (21:7). And of all the male disciples, he is the only one the evangelist records as standing by the cross of Jesus unto the end. It is clear, then, that if the evangelist is highlighting the role of this disciple, it is because he is the hero disciple, the one whose response to Jesus is more profound than any other because it is rooted in a keen awareness of how much he is loved by the Lord. His role in the Calvary scene, we may infer, is a manifestation of Jesus' great love for him as well as his own response in faith. It is not too much to say that he is *the* disciple (the only one in the gospel who is thus described in the singular absolute). Known not by a personal name but simply and symbolically "the disciple whom Jesus loved," he is for all disciples representative and model.[3]

The Mother of Jesus

The central woman in the scene is clearly the mother of Jesus. The mention of the other women standing by the cross reflects the tradition which we know from the synoptic gospels as well, that there was a handful of women followers of Jesus who were faithful to him unto the end (Mk 15:40-41; Mt 27:55-56; Lk 23:27-31). This is probably simply an historical reminiscence without any symbolic value for John. But with the mother of Jesus the case is different. In John's gospel she is never called by her name, Mary. Like the beloved disciple himself, she is named only in terms of her relationship to Jesus. Her identity is simply to be the *Mother of Jesus.*

But Jesus addresses her neither as Mary nor as mother. He calls her "Woman." To our western ear the address "woman" has a ring of disrespect. It was not so in Jesus' day. It was the usual way a man would address a woman, particularly his wife. But it was *not* the customary way for a man to address his mother, and Jesus' rupture of custom here, as at Cana, alerts us to a new meaning. Is is that Jesus is distancing himself from his natural relationship with Mary, reinforcing the synoptic teaching on the superiority of the spiritual relationship to him over natural ties (Mk 3:31; Mt 12:46-50; Lk 8:19-21)? If so, then the address here emphasizes more than ever the real spiritual relationship that is now being established between Mary and the beloved disciple.

However, this scene is central and climactic, and, when combined with Cana, which it echoes, it suggests a much deeper symbolism in the title "woman." In the Genesis story of the primeval couple, "the woman" (named Eve by her husband only later), plays a key role not only in the primal sin but also in the promise of redemption. God's judgment upon the serpent contains a promise of ultimate victory by the woman through her offspring: "I will put enmity between you and the woman, and between your offspring and hers; he will strike at your head, while you strike at his heel" (Gen 3:15). Jesus is the offspring of the *woman*, and by naming Mary with this title, Jesus is suggesting that the earliest promise of salvation is now being fulfilled. Calvary is "his hour" when Satan, the "ruler of this world" is condemned and cast out (Jn 12:31; 14:30; 16:11).

The same biblical imagery lies behind Revelation 12:1-17, where in typical apocalyptic style, the historical events of redemption on earth are interpreted as the counterpart of a heavenly warfare. The seer portrays a great sign in heaven: the woman clothed with the sun, the moon under her feet, and on her head a crown of twelve stars. She labors in childbirth and brings forth the child who is "destined to shepherd all the nations." Satan intervenes to battle the woman, but he is cast down. Who is this woman? As mother of the Messiah, the most obvious answer is Mary. But many of the details of the story suggest that she is also faithful Israel of old who brings forth the Messiah *and* the persecuted church that remains on earth after Jesus' ascension (12:10-18). We shall return to these matters below. For the moment it suffices to note that in the Calvary scene and in Revelation 12, there is the motif of the conquest of Satan through the woman's son.

Spiritual Generation

But there is more at issue here than simply the woman's physical generation of the Messiah. There is a real spiritual begetting of the "rest of her offspring" (Rev 12:17), and to show this we must take three steps: (1) The begetting of the new children of God is a major theme of John's gospel; (2) In the Old Testament imagery exploited by John, Jerusalem is mother of the new generation of God's children; (3) John actualizes Mother Jerusalem in the person of Mary and her new children in the person of

118

the beloved disciple who is proclaimed her son by Jesus from the cross.

a. **Spiritual Begetting in John's Gospel**

The theme of the "kingdom of God" is rare in the fourth gospel. It appears only in Jesus' dialogue with Nicodemus, and there, interestingly enough, in connection with the theme which almost totally replaces it: the divine generation from on high. "No one can see the kingdom of God without being born from above" (3:3). And "No one can enter the kingdom of God without being born of water and Spirit" (3:5). For John, the term *adoption,* used by Paul (Gal 4:5; Rom 8:23), is not strong enough to portray how real the new life of filiation to the Father is. We are *not only* called his children. Such we *are* (1 John 3:1-2). The imagery is even more daring in 1 John 3:9: ". . . God's *seed* remains in him; he cannot sin because he is *begotten by God.*"

But the most significant text is in the prologue, which, if arranged symmetrically,[4] holds as its keystone not "the Word was made flesh and dwelt among us," the description of the Incarnation, which we would normally think to be most important, but rather the preceding verses 12-13:

> To those who did accept him he gave power to become children of God, to those who believe in his name, who were born not by natural generation nor by human choice nor by a man's decision, but of God.

The highlighted message is the divine begetting of the children of God. Is it a coincidence that the symmetrical center of the prologue and the calvary drama treat of the same theme of filiation? At first sight, one might object that the two filiations are different—the one in the prologue to God, the one on Calvary to Mary. However, if we examine John 20:17, we will see that the paschal mystery of Jesus' death and resurrection has effected both a new relationship of the disciples with the Father and with Jesus:

> Go to my *brothers* [and sisters] and tell them, "I am going to my Father and your Father, to my God and your God" (John 20:17).

The disciples, who have been called Jesus' friends in John 15:15 are now called his brothers, because Jesus' father is now their father. What happens in this preascension scene of John 20:17 is anticipated in the Calvary scene, when Jesus, by proclaiming Mary now the mother of the beloved disciple, proclaims by the same gesture that the disciple is Jesus' brother. The divine begetting and Mary's spiritual motherhood are the result of one and the same saving act. As a result of Jesus' death and resurrection, God is now the disciples' Father, and Mary their mother.

b. **Mother Jerusalem**

But where did this woman's role in the divine begetting come from? From two streams of the tradition, one from the Scriptures, the other from the New Testament event.

In the Old Testament, as we have already seen, Jerusalem, portrayed as a woman, is metonomy for the entire people. She is "daughter Jerusalem," "daughter Zion," "virgin daughter," and—important for our inquiry here—mother. If even a gentile people and its capital city can be imaged as mother, as Isaiah does for

120

Sidon (Is 23:4) and Jeremiah for Babylon (Jer 50:12), all the more so can the image be used for Israel and Jerusalem. If the prophets at times use the mother metaphor to accuse the people of infidelity (Hos 2:4), meriting divorce and exile (Is 50:1), the psalmist elsewhere sings with joy and pride that Jerusalem is mother of all. This poetic view appears in Psalm 87. A great festival has drawn seas of pilgrims into the streets of Jerusalem:

> Glorious things are said of you;,
>   O city of God!
> I tell of Egypt and Babylon
>   among those that know the LORD;
> Of Philistia, Tyre, Ethiopia:
>   "This man was born there."
> And of Zion they shall say:
>   "One and all were born in her;
> And he who has established her;
>   is the Most High LORD.
> They shall note, when the peoples are enrolled:
>   "This man was born there."
> And all shall sing, in their festive dance:
>   "My home is within you" (Psalm 87:3-7).

Some scholars think the names of Israel's neighbors refer to diaspora Jews or proselytes who have come from these lands for the feast, the thought being that although physically born in another country, their real home and their real mother is Jerusalem, because their faith makes them one with the children of Israel. Such scholars generally opine for a late date to the psalm, at a period when proselytism was more active among the Jews. Others think the psalm is of much earlier vintage, and they see the poet envisioning, in a flash of inspired universalism, all nations coming to Jerusalem and proclaiming, by embracing the

121

one faith in the one God, that they have all been born in her. We think the latter more likely, for it corresponds to the dreams of other poets and prophets of the Old Testament (Is 2:2-4; 11:10; 18:7; 19:18-24). In any case, Jerusalem is imaged as mother of a vast people, a promise which Christian tradition has understood as fulfilled in the universal church.

But mothers also weep for their children, and thus the mother metaphor is also used for the destruction of Jerusalem and the ensuing exile. Already used by Jeremiah for the destruction and exile of the northern kingdom (Rachel weeping for her lost children, Jer 31:15), the image returns to the author of the Lamentations, as mother Jerusalem cries out: "At this I weep, my eyes run with tears . . . My sons were reduced to silence when the enemy prevailed" (Lam 1:16). Second Isaiah recalls how mother Jerusalem was bereft of children (Is 51:18-20). And in the long prophetic discourse of Baruch 4:5-29, mother Jerusalem addresses her children, recounting first how she fostered them with joy, then with mourning and lament saw them go into exile; but she has trusted in God for their welfare and now rejoices at the coming salvation when her children will be returned to her.

The same image is exploited by the author of the apocryphal Fourth Ezra, a Jewish work written around 100 A.D. (about the same time as John's gospel), and using the ancient imagery to deal with the destruction of Jerusalem by the Romans in 70 A.D. The seer has a vision of a woman:

> . . . and behold, she was mourning and weeping with a loud voice, and was deeply grieved at heart, and her clothes were rent, and there were ashes on her

head. I . . . said to her, "Why are you weeping, and why are you grieved at heart?"

"Let me alone, my lord," she said, "that I may weep for myself and continue to mourn, for I am greatly embittered in spirit and deeply afflicted."

And I said to her, "What has happened to you? Tell me."

The woman then details the source of her grief, the death of her son on the very day of his marriage feast. The seer, thinking the woman is merely an individual mother weeping over her son, while the whole nation is weeping over its destruction, responds to her in anger:

> You most foolish of women, do you not see our mourning, and what has happened to us? For *Zion, the mother of us all,* is in deep grief and great humiliation . . . You are sorrowing for one son, but we, the whole world, for our mother . . . Who then ought to mourn the more, she who lost so great a multitude, or you who are grieving for one?

In the midst of his discourse to the woman, she is suddenly transformed:

> Behold, the woman was no longer visible to me, but there was an established city, and a place of huge foundations showed itself. . .

The angel Uriel then explains to the seer:

> The woman whom you saw, whom you now behold as an established city, is Zion.[5]

Since this image was so deeply ingrained in the consciousness of Israel, it is not surprising that it should be used in the prophetic dreams of Israel's glorious future. A mother about to bear a child is a universal symbol of hope, which Jung would say is buried in the collective unconscious of all peoples. We have already seen how Israel dreamed of the future Messiah in the arms of his mother. But apart from the longing for the personal Messiah, the maternal image also lent itself beautifully to the promised engendering of the new generation of God's people. Negatively, this is expressed by a lament of Isaiah:

> As a woman about to give birth
>   writhes and cries out in her pains,
>   so were we in your presence, O LORD.
> We conceived and writhed in pain,
>   giving birth to wind;
> Salvation we have not achieved for the earth,
>   the inhabitants of the world cannot bring it forth
>   (Is 26:17-18).

Positively, however, Second Isaiah hails the postexilic renewal of Israel in maternal terms:

> Though you were laid waste and desolate,
>   a land of ruins,
> Now you shall be too small for your inhabitants,...
> The children whom you had lost
>   shall yet say to you,
> "This place is too small for me,
>   make room for me to live in."
> You shall ask yourself:
>   Who has borne me these?
> I was bereft and barren [exiled and repudiated];
>   who has reared them?
> I was left all alone;
>   where then do these come from?" (Is 49:19-21)

And again:

> Raise a glad cry, you barren one who did not bear,

break forth in jubilant song, you who were not in
labor,

For more numerous are the children of the deserted
wife than the children of her who has a husband,
says the LORD (Is 54:1).

The climactic text, however, is the one we cited in full
in a previous chapter from Third Isaiah. The surprising
visitation of God's grace enables Zion to bring forth the
new generation speedily:

Before she comes to labor,
    she gives birth;
Before the pains come upon her,
    she safely delivers a male child.
Who ever heard of such a thing,
    or saw the like?
Can a country be brought forth in one day,
    or a nation be born in a single moment?
Yet Zion is scarcely in labor
    when she gives birth to her children (Is 66:7-8).

Notice that the "male child" (singular) is, according to
Hebrew parallelism, equivalent to "country," "nation"
and "children." This "overlay" of singular and plural
perhaps helps us to understand how Mary's motherhood
can be both singular (Jesus/the beloved disciple) and
collective (the disciples).

The text continues:

Shall I bring a mother to the point of birth,
    and yet not let her child be born? says the LORD.
Or shall I allow her to conceive,
    yet close her womb? says your God. [Again a
return to the singular.]

Rejoice with Jerusalem and be glad because of her,
    all you who love her;
Exult, exult with her,
    all you who were mourning over her!
    Oh, that you may suck fully
    of the milk of her comfort,
That you may nurse with delight
    at her abundant breasts!...
As nurslings, you shall be carried in her arms,
    and fondled in her lap;
As a mother comforts her son,
    so will I comfort you;
    in Jerusalem you shall find your comfort
    (Is 66:9-13).

c. **Mother Zion is Mary**

It is clear that Jesus' confiding of Mary to the beloved disciple is not merely a son's provision for his mother's care after his death. What Jesus does here is the fulfillment of prophecy, for the very next verse states that Jesus "seeing now that all things had been accomplished. . ." (19:28). The unusual title "Woman" by which Jesus addresses his mother leads us to the woman of Genesis 3:15, which spoke of the "seed" of the woman who would engage Satan. But the prophecies which the announcement of Jesus most clearly fulfill are those foretelling the generation of the new people of God by mother Jerusalem. The surprise is that the fufillment goes beyond expectations, for there is a real human mother who fulfills the promises, who is Jerusalem in person.

She is *faithful* Jerusalem. There is such a strong indictment in John of unfaithful Israel, embodied in the leaders who rejected Jesus, that the reader may well wonder if

126

there is any continuity left with the old. There is. To faithless Jerusalem John provides a contrasting embodiment of faithful Jerusalem in the faithful woman at the foot of the cross. And what more natural choice for the fulfillment of the promises of Mother Zion than she who was also mother of the Messiah himself, Jesus, whose saving death and resurrection now multiplies himself in a collectivity of brothers and sisters ("Go to my brothers and tell them. . ." John 20:17)—a mystery Paul puts in other words: God's plan was that Jesus "might be the firstborn of many brothers" (Rom 8:29) and the prophet John describes as the "other children" of the woman who brought forth the Messiah (Rev 12:17). Although *4 Ezra* is a Jewish writing, its author was a contemporary of the fourth Evangelist and tributary to the same tradition of Mother Zion. Borrowing his graphic imagery, we could say that the individual woman he saw, who then was transformed into a city, came full circle when John transformed the city again into an individual woman, Mary, the mother of Jesus now become the mother of the disciples.

Jesus

The principal actor in this scene is Jesus himself. The central action is Jesus' transfer of gifts—Mary to the disciple, the disciple to Mary. During his ministry Jesus bestowed many gifts: his word, his signs, the Eucharist, the revelation of the Father. As a person in the shadow of impending death gives away, one by one, his personal treasures to the survivors whom he loves most dearly, so does Jesus at his "hour." It is his final gift before he dies, given with utter freedom. The soldiers take his clothes and divide them; it was not his choice who would receive them. Not so with the gift of his mother, Jesus' last initiative before he breathes his last. His mother is not taken from him; he gives her away.

The Disciple Took Her. . .

"From that hour" does not mean mere chronological time. In John the "hour" refers to the supreme moment of Jesus' self-gift, the hour of his passion, that hour already alluded to in the wedding feast of Cana, "My hour has not yet come" (2:4). The new relationship is made possible by Jesus' own saving act.

The mother of Jesus no doubt accepts the gift of her new son and in him all other disciples. Perhaps this detail was so obvious that the evangelist saw no need to record it. What was important to record, however, was that the disciple *took her into his own.* In John the word "took" has different meanings. When the object is an inanimate thing, the verb has the normal active sense of "take," as, e.g., when Jesus "took the loaves" (6:11). When the object of the verb is a gift or a blessing, the word means "to receive" (e.g. grace, l:16; the Spirit, 7:39; 14:17; what we ask for in prayer, 16:24). In John, when the object of the verb is a person or his message (repeatedly used for receiving Jesus: 1:12; 5:43; 13:20), the meaning is really "to welcome." In saying therefore that the disciple took her, the evangelist wishes to express the free, conscious and wholehearted response of the beloved disciple to the gift, the joyful welcome he gives her.

The fourth gospel is strewn with examples of people who are offered Jesus' precious gifts but are too obtuse to receive them. Even the disciples do not fully realize the overwhelming gift which Jesus is giving at each new turn of his ministry, and some, at the promise of the

128

Eucharist, turn away completely (6:66). But the beloved disciple here, as elsewhere, is outstanding in his insight and response. He realizes how much the gift of Jesus' own mother is a mark of Jesus' special love for him.

He takes her *into his own*. Sometimes this is translated "into his home" or "into his care." The Greek literally reads, "into the things that were his own." It is doubtful in biblical and even in profane Greek that this expression means "took her into his home."[6] Given John's use of it elsewhere in his gospel, the expression has a deeper meaning in keeping with the symbolic thrust of the entire passage. *"He came unto his own"* of 1:11 means that the Word came to the people who belonged to him. "His own" in 10:4 refers to the sheep belonging to the good Shepherd. When the devil tells a lie, he "speaks in character"—the New American Revised New Testament translation for "he speaks from what is his own"' (8:44), as the world would love "what is its own" (15:19). Finally, when Jesus is said to "love his own," the evangelist is underlining the intense communion between Jesus and his disciples. Hence, here in the Calvary scene the meaning to be preferred is "the things he treasured, the spiritual space which the beloved disciple made for the gifts of the Lord." The sentence means, then, that the disciple took the mother of Jesus into the home of his heart, holding and caring for her there as a most precious treasure.

Have We Welcomed Her?

Clearly the beloved disciple is being held up as a model of response to Jesus. He is such because he responds with deep and grateful awareness to the person and the gifts of Jesus. The text then is a clear invitation to the church and to each of its members to follow the disciple's example and to receive the gift of Mary from Jesus on the cross. In the Christian life, it is possible to journey for many years before coming to the moment of "awakening" to a treasure that is already there, but not consciously owned. The Peace Corps volunteer in Chapter 3 speaks of discovering the Eucharist. Many Christians today speak of their discovery of the Holy Spirit—often many, many years after their baptism. From my experiences of preaching or directing retreats on the "Our Father" I know that many Christians, lay, priests and religious, discover the real meaning of *Abba* in their lives not at the beginning of their Christian walk but only at some significant moment of grace later.

It is this progressive "unwrapping" of the treasures of Jesus that Paul describes as the work of the Holy Spirit (1 Cor 2:9-13), the progressive insight and understanding for which the apostle repeatedly prays (Phil 1:9; Eph 1:15-19; 3:14-19):

> . . . that the God of our Lord Jesus Christ, the Father of glory, may give you a spirit of wisdom and revelation resulting in knowledge of him. May the eyes of [your] hearts be enlightened, that you may know what is the hope that belongs to his call, what are the riches of glory in his inheritance among the holy ones, and what is the surpassing greatness of his power for us who believe (Eph 1:17-19).

Now from the Calvary scene it is clear that Mary, the Mother of Jesus, is part of those treasures of Jesus that the Holy Spirit unwraps. One must, of course, be open to the gift, and prayer is the way to that openness. Have you ever consciously received Mary as your mother? Have you every consciously said "Yes" to this gift? Far from

130

being a threat to Jesus, when you receive his gifts, you receive him in a deeper way.

Consecration to Mary?

Let us now look at the practice, promoted by St. Louis Grignion de Montfort, Ven. William Joseph Chaminade and others, of "consecrating" oneself to Mary. Theologically there is a difficulty here, because consecration is an act of religion by which we set something or someone aside for *God*. Strictly speaking, one can consecrate only to God. When a church or a chalice is consecrated, it is withdrawn from profane use and dedicated to the service of God alone. By baptism we have been consecrated to God in union with Christ:

> You were consecrated, you were justified in the name of the Lord Jesus Christ and in the Spirit of our God (1 Cor 6:11 my translation).

And the result is that the Christian as well as the church is a temple of the living God (1 Cor 6:19; 3:16-17).

But where does this consecration come from? Not from some humanly devised initiative. Biblically speaking, man never consecrates himself. What is undertaken simply on his own initiative is of no value in the eyes of God. "It is obedience that I ask for and not sacrifice" (1 Sam 15:22; Hos 6:6). Man's attempt to approach God on his own is ironically caricatured in the building of the tower of Babel, which not only failed to reach God but also disintegrated human relationships (Gen 11:1-9). No, the initiative for genuine consecration must come from God himself. The prophets of Baal screamed and gashed themselves for a whole day, but no fire came from heaven to consume the offerings. It was the Lord's free decision

131

to send fire to consume the victims Elijah has prepared (1 Kgs 18).

For the Christian, the "holy one of God" (Mk 1:245), the one the Father consecrated and sent into the world (Jn 10:36), is Jesus. Any other genuine consecration can only be an extension and participation in his. "For these I consecrate myself, that they may be consecrated in truth" (Jn 17:19). In other words, the "structure" of consecration is one that depends upon God's free initiative and must follow carefully the strategy he himself has laid out for such consecration. It can only be a response to the consecrating action of God, which is basically his gift in Christ Jesus.

Now it is also obvious that Jesus mediates his holiness, his consecration, through various gifts—his word, his Spirit, Baptism, the Eucharist—and when one receives in conscious faith any of Jesus' gifts, he or she is thereby consecrated, participating in the very consecration of Jesus himself. Consecration happens through obedient surrender in faith to the plan and the gifts of God. And consecration is not just a once-done act; begun as a consecration in baptism, the Christian life grows in ever deeper consecration, ever deeper belonging, to God. Thus to Christians already well under way Paul writes:

> May the God of peace consecrate you through and through,[7] and may your whole being, spirit, soul and body be kept blameless for the coming of our Lord Jesus Christ (1 Thes 5:23 my translation).

This progressive work of sanctification (another word for consecration) God mediates through his gifts, and we yield to the divine action by responding to them.

Mary is clearly one of the gifts of Jesus. To welcome her as our mother is to receive the consecrating action of God. We enter more deeply into the holiness of God by accepting this gift. The bond which God establishes between Mary and us, a bond of mother and child, when affirmed and accepted by us, is a new and deeper consecration of ourselves *to God.*

In the sacrament of matrimony, one person makes a covenant with the other, giving oneself and receiving the gift of the other. The partners do not consecrate themselves to each other, nor even to God. Through the sacrament God consecrates the bond they have formed with each other and thereby "consecrates" them to himself. In an analogous way, to accept the gift of Mary, to enter consciously into a filial covenant with her, is to be consecrated more deeply to God through accepting his gift. The obvious differences from marriage are that, as Mary is Jesus' mother, the bond is a maternal-filial one offered to all disciples of Jesus, and the gift is more directly connected with spiritual transformation into Jesus, as we shall see in the next chapter.

These reflections suffice to show in what sense one may speak of "consecration to Mary." The term suggests a positive initiative on the part of the Christian, and to that extent it echoes the beloved disciple's conscious *taking* of Mary as his mother. However, the aspect that is easily neglected, and often in fact bypassed in an unenlightened casual use of "consecration to Mary," is by far the more important one, that Mary is first of all God's gift offered by Jesus from the cross. God offers us a consecrating gift, and our acceptance of that gift of Mary, allows God to consecrate us more fully to himself.

One may ask then, whether the term "consecration to Mary" really conveys the richness of this mystery.[8] "Marian consecration" has been offered as an alternative. Pope John Paul II, who states that the reading of St. Louis de Montfort's *True Devotion to Mary* "marked a decisive turning point in my life,"[9] and whose Marian motto *Totus Tuus* comes from the Saint, has used the word *entrustment* or *entrusting* (official translation of *affidamento*) in his invitiation to all the bishops of the world to consecrate themselves and their dioceses to Mary on March 25, 1984. The official English title of the text was: "Act of Entrusting to Our Lady."[10]

I do not propose to resolve the question of words here. What I do offer is a formula, based on the Calvary scene, which I have used in my personal prayer for years and others have found helpful:

> Lord Jesus,
> To the disciple whom you loved
> You gave Mary, your Mother,
> As your final gift before you died,
> That she should be his mother and mine.
> As the beloved disciple took her to be his own,
> So I now take her as my mother.
> Under her influence may I be formed
> By the Holy Spirit to your likeness
> And proclaim the gift you continue to make of her
> For the building up of your body, the church,
> To the glory of God the Father. Amen.

If one wishes to use this prayer for community recitation, the singular "I," "my," and "mine" may readily be converted to the plural "we" forms. The last five lines of the prayer announce the theme of the next chapter.

NOTES

1. See R. E. Brown, *The Gospel According to John, xiii-xxi,* Anchor Bible 29A (Garden City: Doubleday, 1970), 948-952.

2. Brown, 911. Brown considers the crucifixion as an introduction, the burial as a conclusion, and he groups verses 23-24, 28-30 and 31-37 as single episodes. As episodic groupings, his arrangement is more accurate. My arrangement has sought to bring out details. In either case, Jesus' gift of his mother to the beloved disciple is the central scene.

3. In an excellent article W. S. Kurz has brought together the fruits of recent significant research, especially in narrative criticism, to show that the omission of the beloved disciple's name, as well as other intentional gaps, point to the symbolic nature of this important character in the fourth gospel and invite the implied reader to identify with him in his various experiences in the latter part of the gospel. The same is true of the mother of Jesus, the intentional omission of whose name reinforces her symbolic character. The situation of contemporary Christians who spontaneously identify with what happens in the narrative and especially "their identification with the beloved disciple is clearly warranted by the text." W. S. Kurz, "The Beloved Disciple and Implied Readers," *Biblical Theology Bulletin* 19 (1989), 100-107.

4. M.-E. Boismard, *St. John's Prologue* (Westminster: Newman, 1957) 73-81.

5. *4 Ezra* 9:38-10:44; J.H. Charlesworth, *The Old Testament Pseudepigrapha,* vol. 1 (Garden City: Doubleday, 1983) 546-547. The Apocalypse of Baruch, dated between 100 and 120 A.D., does not portray mother Jerusalem as weeping but instead, the seer weeps over his destroyed mother: "O Lord, my Lord, have I therefore come into the world to see the evil things of my mother? No, my Lord. If I have found grace in your eyes, take away my spirit first that I may go to my fathers and I may not see the destruction of my mother. For from two sides I am hard pressed: I cannot resist you, but my soul also cannot behold the evil of my mother." *Apoc. Bar.* 3:1-3; Charlesworth, 621.

6. I. de la Potterie, "La parole de Jésus 'Voici ta Mére' et l'accueil du Disciple," *Marianum* 36 (1974), 21-39.

7. The Greek verb *hagiazo,* translated "consecrate" here, can also be rendered "sanctify," "make holy," "hallow." *Today's English Version* translates, "make you completely his." In any case, the text envisions a *progress* in the state in which one was constituted by one's baptismal consecration.

8. In justice to St. Louis de Montfort, it must be said that although he does use the term "consecration to Mary," it is clear from a study of his writings that he considers the act to be Christocentric and Trinitarian, a renewal and deepening of the Christian's baptismal consecration and therefore a formal

act of worship of God, *latria. True Devotion,* 120. Cf. J. P. Gaffney, S.M.M., "St. Louis Grignion de Montfort and the Marian Consecration," *Marian Studies 35* (1984) 147-150.

9. A. Frossard, *N'ayez pas peur: dialogues avec Jean Paul II* (Paris: Editions Robert Laffont, 1982), 184.

10. Official text in *L'Osservatore Romano* 124 (18 Feb. 1984).

Chapter Seven

OUR FATHER, OUR MOTHER

Mary, Instrument of the Holy Spirit

In the previous chapters we explored three biblical motifs which reach their perfection in the person of Mary. Two basic facets of Mary's role emerge. She is model of response to the good news, and she is mother not only of the Messiah but of the community of believers. The Holy Spirit continues to use these motifs and functions of Mary in the ongoing spiritual formation of the church and of the individual disciple. St. Paul makes clear that the progressive transformation into Christ is the work of the Holy Spirit:

> We all with faces unveiled, reflecting [or "contemplating"] as in a mirror the glory of the Lord, are being transformed into his very image by the Spirit of the Lord (2 Cor 3:18 my translation).

137

In this work of progressive transformation, Mary is not a late appendage dreamed up by the Christian piety of later centuries. She is an instrument of the Holy Spirit from the very beginning, not merely in the birthing and human formation of Jesus but in the spiritual formation of the church. The Holy Spirit surely uses other instruments—the word of God, the preaching of the church, the sacraments. But in the Holy Spirit's quiver of tools, there is none more powerful than the example of the saints, and here the mother of Jesus has the primordial place. She is not a metaphor but a revealing symbol in person.[1] She exemplifies total surrender to the plan of God, a surrender that is not passivity but activation of all her powers. She is not a symbol for the subjugation of women to men; she is the symbol of the submission of every Christian and of the church as a whole to God. And though not divine, she mediates the maternal love and consolation of God, fulfilling that function prophesied for mother Jerusalem (Is 66:13).[2]

Little wonder then that Christians should find the companionship of Mary a powerful stimulus and guide to their growth in faith. Little wonder that Christians who have not had a devotion to Mary from their childhood, as well as those who have, often speak of discovering the gift of Mary in their lives. If Mary is the spouse of the Holy Spirit, then she is not a relic of his past work but an instrument of his ongoing work in the life of every disciple of Jesus. If some Christians even speak of experiencing a presence of Mary, this presence is not an outer, corporeal one, but rather an inner, but no less real, presence mediated by the Holy Spirit—for a purpose. The Holy Spirit brings to life all that belongs to Jesus: "He will receive of what is mine and declare it to you" (John

16:15). When the Holy Spirit brings alive the gift of Jesus' mother, when the disciple consciously welcomes Mary as his or her mother, then a powerful new dimension has opened up in the disciple's life, a lifegiving treasure.

But this is a grace. No amount of discussion or study will produce the experience; it can only be prayed for. Yet, inasmuch as it is one of the gifts Jesus wills for the disciples whom he loves, it is surely one easily obtained by prayer.

The Fatherhood of God and the Motherhood of Mary

Since Mary is Jesus' gift to us, she relates us immediately to him as giver of the gift and as our elder brother. That is easily seen. What is less often perceived is that Mary's maternal love and influence is not a complement or balance to the Father's love. Even less is it the "back door of mercy" in contrast to the "front door of justice" (a homiletical trick that is a theological absurdity). Her love is rather the *instrument of the God's own maternal love,* which was only implicit in the biblical term "Father" but is clearly and beautifully mediated in a unique way through Mary. She is not a metaphorical appendage but a revelation in person of the maternal face of God. There is nothing Mary has that she has not received. Her maternal love is first of all God's love for us. If, in the historical tradition that has come down to us, God has chosen to be known as *Abba* and to allow the overflowing maternal dimension of that love to be mediated through Mary, it would seem most fruitful to follow the revealed pattern and to allow God to exercise his mothering of us through her rather than trying to introject a functional motherhood or title "Mother" into the Godhead, however theoretically valid that might be. It would seem

139

best, in other words, to go to God as he has chosen to come to us.[3]

Jesus, whose mother was Mary, called God "Abba," and it was Mary, not God, whom he called "Imma." And it was Mary, not God, whom he told us to call "Mother." That fact is the ultimate reason for retaining, in its rich and overflowing biblical meaning, the title "Father" for God, and fully exploiting, for its spiritual power, the title "Mother" for Mary. Those who think this "less perfect" would do well to reflect on this: Jesus gave us the title Abba to express both the transcendence and the intimacy of God. For the maternal face of God he did not leave us a title. He left us instead a living symbol, a human person, a human mother. She is of our earth, born into the constraints of time and space, a journeyer in faith, overwhelmed by the mystery of God's action in her life, rejoicing and sorrowing as any human might, the supreme model of how the transcendent God is to be experienced in the immanence of ordinary daily life. Yet now by the gift of the Spirit she is elevated and enabled to mother each of us personally in such a way that she genuinely reveals and mediates God's own maternal love for us. *To reveal his maternal face God chose not a maternal title but a human mother.* To address God directly as "Mother" therefore turns out to be not an advance but an impoverishment of the treasure of revelation already given us. "Mother" means closeness. The wedding of heaven and earth, God and humanity, took place when God brought forth his Son through an earthly mother, the same mother he gives to us. An unseen "divine mother" would be more remote than the "close" woman who shares our nature and makes "divine maternity" humanly understandable.

140

We are now in a position to evaluate the objection raised by some feminists that using "Father" alone for God implies that women are inferior to men, that motherhood is inferior to fatherhood. Revelation, particularly the New Testament, affirms the fundamental equality of man and woman. The image of God in which humanity is created is male and female (Genesis 1:26). And in the order of redemption there is "neither male nor female. You are all one in Christ Jesus" (Galatians 3:28). But from this principle of equality does it follow that the *symbolic* roles of man and woman are *identical?* The basic biological differences of the sexes, prolonged in psychological and expecially parental differences, indicate otherwise. While both are called to be loving, strong, faithful, caring, and to fulfill all the other virtuous functions for the child, each fulfills these in ways appropriate to his or her sex. The father represents the "far world," the mother the "near world," and the happy complementarity of this interaction on the child assures its healthy psychosocial development. For this reason, "father" is a more adequate symbol of the transcendence, the otherness of God, while "mother" translates immanence, closeness. In the Christian tradition, while God's immanence in creation supposes this transcendence, his transcendence does not demand immanence, for God did not *have* to create the world. It was his free choice to do so. Therefore it is theologically important to keep the priority of God's transcendence because it is the foundation of his freely chosen immanence. In this, although we obviously must be aware of the limitations of our metaphorical language, "father" becomes a more appropriate title than "mother."

In the order of redemption, the incarnation is the supreme act of God's condescending mercy, his gift by which he freely chooses to bridge the infinite abyss between God and man. And here the achievement of the marvelous closeness is done through a human mother, who is not only the mother of the incarnate Savior but is made by God to be mother of all. Such an initiative on God's part certainly reveals the maternal aspect of his love. But also, by avoiding the confusion of a maternal title *within* God, it preserves and heightens the transcendence of God symbolized by the title "Father." At the same time it immeasurably dignifies womanhood, for no human person was ever so close both to God and humanity as the woman, Mary. And it was through a woman that the whole "drawing near" of God was consummated, culminating in the revelation of his face as "Abba."

"I will not leave you orphans," Jesus said (Jn 14:18). An orphan has neither father nor mother. Jesus gave us both: "No one has ever seen God. The only son, God, who is at the Father's side, has revealed him" (Jn 1:18). And: "Behold your mother" (Jn 19:27). We can live as orphans if we choose. But we can also claim our birthright and live as children nurtured to fullness by a father's and a mother's love.

NOTES

1. J E. Schillebeeckx, *Mary, Mother of the Redemption,* tr. N. D. Smith (New York: Sheed and Ward, 1964), 109-110.

2. Following the lead of St. Maximilian Kolbe, Leonardo Boff proposes that Mary is "hypostatically assumed" or "hypostatically united" to the Holy Spirit (*The Maternal Face,* 93, 256). Because this is also the terminology used for the incarnation of the Word, it appears to me too adventuresome to use of Mary, who always remains a human person, nor does it seem necessary to describe the exalted role she continues to play as the instrument of the Holy Spirit.

3. I find it significant that Leonardo Boff in discussing *The Feminine Face of God,* though holding that God is also (and even "above all") mother, considers Mary to be the supreme revelation of the feminine in God and does not even raise the question of the appropriateness of the traditional title "Father" for God.

Appendix A

"WHO AM I THAT THE MOTHER OF MY LORD SHOULD COME TO ME?"

A TESTIMONY BY PATTI MANSFIELD[1]

Patti Gallagher Mansfield was one of the Duquesne University students with whom the charismatic renewal began in the Catholic Church in 1967. Married and the mother of four children, she is a leader in the renewal, an inspiring conference speaker, monthly columnist in New Covenant magazine, and author of *Proclaim His Marvelous Deeds*. At my request, she has written the following testimony, which I gratefully offer here for many of its insights, not the least of which is the relationship Patti has experienced in her own life between the Holy Spirit and the mother of Jesus.

Mary, Spouse of the Holy Spirit

As a teenager, surrounded by Jewish friends, I felt a growing need to understand my own faith better. For this reason I decided on a Catholic university, Duquesne in Pittsburgh. I took some theology, began attending daily Mass and joined a Scripture study group called *Chi Rho*. It was this *Chi Rho* group that made a retreat February 17-19, which marked the beginning of the charismatic renewal in the Catholic church.

About twenty-five students met with our faculty advisors and chaplain to spend a weekend in prayer, focusing on the person and work of the Holy Spirit. Friday night we began with a meditation on Mary. The theology professor giving the talk held up a statue of Mary with her hands raised in prayer. He described her as a woman of faith and a woman of prayer. As he spoke about Our Lady that night, I could tell that something had happened to him. In class he had always been high strung and nervous. Yet that night, when he spoke about Mary there was a peace and calm about him. "Spirit-filled" was the term that kept coming to my mind to describe his new disposition. What I didn't know then was that he and a few other professors from Duquesne had attended an interdenominational prayer group just a few weeks before. There they had received what we now call the "baptism of the Holy Spirit." I was witnessing the fruit of his experience as he spoke about Mary with such faith and power.

My conversion took place during that retreat. I went into the chapel, not to pray, but to tell any students there to come down to a birthday party for some of our members. As I knelt in the presence of Jesus in the Blessed Sacrament, I trembled with a sense of the majesty of God. He is the King of Kings and Lord of Lords. Even though I was afraid, I remained in his presence and prayed a prayer of unconditional surrender: "Father, whatever you want from my life, I say 'yes' to it. If it means suffering, I'll accept it. Just teach me how to follow Jesus, your Son, and to love the way he loves." As I prayed that prayer I was kneeling, and the next moment I found myself prostrate before Jesus in the Blessed Sacrament. I was flooded with a tremendous sense of God's personal love for me. The words of St. Augustine best capture what I experienced in those moments: "You have made us for yourself, O Lord, and our hearts are restless until they rest in you."

Over the next hour God's Spirit was so sovereignly poured out on the group that all the young people who were at the party downstairs were drawn up into the chapel. As we knelt there, some people wept. Others laughed for joy. Still others raised their hands in prayer. We had been immersed in the Spirit of the living God. The grace poured out upon us that weekend has over-flowed into the lives of literally millions of Catholics the world over. The birthday party was symbolic, for that day marked the birth of the charismatic renewal in the Catholic church.

And who ordinarily plans and prepares a birthday party for her children? Mary had been there at the beginning of the retreat, and she was in that upper room the next night when the Holy Spirit came upon us, just as she had been at the first Pentecost.

That realization dawned on me in what happened next. From the chapel I went to my room and opened the Scripture at random. I didn't know much about the Bible. I certainly had never opened the Scripture expecting to receive a personal word from God. But that night I did. These are the words my eyes fell upon:

> My soul magnifies the Lord and my spirit rejoices in God my Savior, because he has regarded the low estate of his handmaiden. For behold henceforth all generations will call me blessed. For he who is mighty has done great things for me, and holy is his Name, and his mercy is from age to age on those who fear him. He has shown strength with his arm. He has scattered the proud in the imagination of their hearts. He has put down the mighty from their thrones and exalted those of low degree. He has filled the hungry with good things, and the rich he has sent empty away. He has helped his servant Israel in remembrance of his mercy, as he spoke to our fathers, to Abraham and his posterity forever (Luke 1:46-55 RSV).

God allowed me to receive the words of Mary our Mother as the very first personal word he ever spoke to me. Every time, for more than twenty years, when I have shared the story of what happened at Duquesne, I have always included the Magnificat. From that very first moment I knew I was caught up in the mystery of Mary's response to God. Her Magnificat has overflowed into my life and now it is my own Magnificat. The "yes" that she said to God at the Annunciation has become my "yes."

Honor Your Mother

Many who have had a conversion experience find such joy in relating to the person of Jesus Christ, they see no need for Mary and the saints. After my experience at Duquesne I too entered into a new intimacy with the Lord in prayer, in his word and in the sacraments. But as my relationship with Jesus deepened, so did my love for Mary.

How could this be? The Lord showed me in a simple way during a visit by my mother after the birth of our second child. My mother cooked, cleaned, and gave lots of encouragement. "Your mother is so loving," commented my husband one day. "She really has a servant's heart. Now I see for myself why you think she's special."

I was happy that two people I love so much were coming to know and love each other as well. A lesson was beginning to unfold for me.

Mother's birthday occurred during her visit with us that year. In the midst of all the preparations for my new baby, I had neglected to get her a gift. My husband bought her something, but I felt sad that I had nothing for her myself. There was little I could do to serve her, for she was serving me.

But when Mother's birthday arrived something wonderful happened. Two of my friends, without a word from me, remembered her birthday. One prepared a delicious birthday meal and delivered it piping hot. The other brought her a beautiful card and gift. These friends had already cooked for me and given me gifts. Now they were honoring my mother.

Mother was amazed. "Why are your friends doing this

when they hardly know me? It must be out of love for you." To be sure, love for my mother was love for me. Honor for her was really honor for me. How grateful I was to my friends! How much more I loved them for loving my mother. Suddenly I was caught up in the relationship of another mother and child. From the cross the Lord said to the beloved disciple, "Behold your mother," and the disciple received Mary into his home. Out of love for Jesus, his friends still receive her today.

I once stood near two women who had never met. The one said, "I'm Johnny's mother." Immediately the other woman embraced her. It was her love for Johnny that spurred her to welcome his mother with such enthusiasm. To honor Johnny's mother was to honor Johnny. It's because of Jesus that we enter into a relationship with Mary.

Mama

But our relationship with Mary is meant to go much deeper than honor. I know many people who respect and honor their mothers but feel little personal warmth or closeness to them. I believe the Lord wants all his children to experience Mary's motherly love so that we may turn to her with confidence in our need. A kind of "bonding" needs to take place as with any mother and child.

Just as I set out to share these thoughts, my baby Patrick began to call for me with a long string of "Mamamama's." When each of my children started to talk, they happily babbled their "Dadadada" sounds all day. But when they were tired, hungry, frightened or hurt they used a different syllable. Instinctively they knew that "Mama" was another word for help. Simple as it is, the cry for help and the helping that follows is how bonding grows between mother and child. So it is not surprising that the bonding between Christians and Mary takes place through cries to her for help. Maybe that is one of the reasons why the Church celebrates the feast of Mary, the Mother of God, on January 1. We are doing more than simply honoring her. We are saying that to get through a new year of our Lord we need the help of the Mother of the Lord, Mary, Mother, "Mama," as Patrick would call her.

Mother of All

Several years ago, while speaking to Catholics on retreat, I encouraged them to seek a closer relationship with Mary. "Ask Jesus to introduce you to his mother," I urged them. Little did I know that one of the retreatants, Sally, was from a Four Square Gospel Church. The idea of relating to Mary was foreign to her, but she wanted to be open. Later, Sally was praying in the chapel. She knew Jesus and loved him very much, so she asked him quite simply, "Introduce me to your mother." Jesus answered her prayer. Sally gives witness that Mary came to her in that chapel, took Sally into her arms and embraced her. From that night on Sally knew she had a mother in heaven who loved her, who understood her struggle, who wanted to help her. As time passed Sally felt gradually drawn into the Catholic church. She is a Catholic today.

While working with the poor, a religious sister I know met a lovely Baptist woman who plied her with questions about Mary. The woman had seen the pilgrim statue of our Lady of Fatima in someone's home and was intrigued. "Do you think Mary would come to my house, Sister?"

"Surely, if you want her," my friend replied. Imagine the surprise of the woman's son, a Baptist minister, when he came for a visit and saw the statue. "Don't say a word about her, Boy. I'm your mother. She's his mother. She stays!" While remaining a Baptist, this simple woman literally welcomed Mary into her home and experienced the power of having a relationship with the mother of Jesus.

A minister I know tells how he had reached an impasse in his prayer life. One day he locked himself in his office, determined not to leave until he had broken through in prayer. The Holy Spirit began to lead him to passages in Scripture that spoke of Mary. This man of God came under conviction that he had not shown enough respect for the mother of the Lord. He repented and determined never again to show dishonor for Mary.

They Have No Wine

In the *Memorare* we pray, "Remember, O most gracious Virgin Mary, that *never* was it known that *anyone* who fled to your protection, implored your help or sought your intercession was left unaided." Never was anyone left unaided!

Mary's role as intercessor in my life is best illustrated in the following story. After my conversion I longed to share with my mom and dad, my two sisters and brother the joy and peace I'd found in surrendering my life to Jesus. I wanted them to experience for themselves the power of being baptized in the Holy Spirit. But it seemed so difficult to lead them into this dimension of Christian living. As I sought the Lord for wisdom, two inspirations came.

The first was to pray in a consistent, determined way for them. In 1968 I heard Ralph Martin share that he had set aside one day a week to intercede for his family. He was praying that each of them might come to know the Lord in a personal way. Encouraged by his example, I too began to pray and sacrifice every Thursday for my family, interceding for a deeper conversion for each one.

The second inspiration came as I was making a visit to the parish where I grew up, Immaculate Heart of Mary, in Maplewood, New Jersey. In an alcove of that church is a life-sized wooden statue of Mary seated with the infant Jesus on her lap. She looks neither frail nor delicate. This beautiful statue portrays Mary as womanly yet strong, worthy of trust, able to care for all those entrusted to her. As I knelt at the altar I felt inspired to entrust every member of my family to Mary. Once I did so a deep peace came over me. I asked her to pray for them unceasingly until each one was fully surrendered to the Lord. "They have no more wine," Mary said at Cana long ago. That simple word from his mother caused Jesus to perform a miracle. I believed she would do it for me.

I prayed and Mary prayed, and within one year my two sisters and my mother were baptized in the Holy Spirit. I'll never forget the day my mother told me she wanted to be baptized in the Spirit. It was after a prayer meeting. I was so thrilled I didn't know what to do! "Wait here, Mom. I'll get someone to talk to you," I blurted. She later told me she was disappointed I didn't offer to pray with her myself.

Five years passed. I continued to pray and entrust my family to Mary. As May 1973 approached I felt a special leading to ask my mother and sisters to join me in praying for my dad. During the month of May we agreed to pray the rosary daily that Daddy be drawn closer to God. On May 4th one of my uncles invited my dad to make a Life in the Spirit Seminar and my dad agreed! We had invited Dad to a seminar many times before and he refused. This was a moment of grace. By God's providence I was able to be home in New Jersey the night my dad was prayed with for the Baptism of the Spirit. He later told me he smelled a distinct aroma of incense—even though no incense was burning—a beautiful sign of the presence of God.

That left only my brother who was not yet baptized in the Spirit. He was a good Catholic but needed a greater personal experience of God's love. We continued to pray. While my brother was jogging, the Lord Jesus appeared to him with arms outstretched. "Come to me, Peter," Jesus beckoned. My brother said that as he began running toward Jesus, the vision faded but he continued to hear the Lord's voice. There on the road he surrendered his life to the Lord and was filled with the Spirit. Imagine my joy when he called me with the news! "I always wanted to be baptized in the Spirit," he said. This was a well kept secret. We never really talked much about it. I was especially touched when I realized that his encounter with the Lord took place on the Feast of Our Lady of Lourdes! A week later some friends laid hands on him in prayer. This was the fifteenth anniversary of my own Baptism in the Spirit. What a wonderful anniversary gift!

Teach Us to Pray

When my son Peter was a toddler, I used to arrange my daily prayer time in the afternoon while he watched Sesame Street. One afternoon as I sat in my rocker, trying to pray, I kept dozing off to sleep. "This will never do,"

I told myself. "Maybe if I kneel I can stay awake." So I knelt, bowed my head to the floor and covered my eyes with my hands. After a few moments of prayer, I sensed a presence near me. It wasn't an angel or an apparition, just my little boy, Peter! As I opened my eyes, there he was, kneeling and bowing in exactly the same manner I was. His hands were folded and he was watching me intently. In a sweet voice he asked, "What are we praying about today, Mom?" Just as little Peter wanted to enter into my prayer, I'm sure the child Jesus was molded by the prayer of his mother.

Mary continues her role as teacher of prayer today. She desires to show us how to take our clenched fists and closed hearts and open them up to God, to let our lives serve his plan.

Totus Tuus

When Al and I were married in December, 1973 (our Gospel was the wedding feast of Cana!) we made an act of consecration of our lives and our marriage to Mary. Each of our four children was consecrated to her at baptism and first Holy Communion. In front of our home stands a statue of our Lady which baby Patrick calls "Mama." He insists on kissing her every time we go out and he makes everyone else kiss her too! (He apparently isn't worried about "pushing" his Marian devotion on others!) Even though Mary had always been important in our lives, we felt called to a new depth of consecration to her in 1979.

That call came to both Al and me when we listened to a recorded talk given by Fr. Francis Martin. It was a scriptural presentation about Mary originally given to priests at a Steubenville Conference. As we played that tape again and again, something happened deep within us. Our relationship with Mary shifted gears. Al said that when he would kneel in chapel to pray, Jesus seemed to draw him to look to Mary. It was as though the Lord had a new lesson for us concerning Mary's place in the salvation of the world.

Not long thereafter we read a book entitled *The Spirit and the Bride Say "Come!"* by Fr. George Kosicki, C.S.B. and Fr. Gerald Farrell, S.M. Fr. George is a dear friend of ours who has helped us grow in love for Jesus and Mary over the years. I feel that this is a prophetic book. It deals with the role of Mary in the new Pentecost, and how God intends to use her to bring about the reign of Jesus in the world today. The bottom line in the book is this: God wants all of us to consecrate our lives to Mary. That consecration is a key to the plan of God unfolding.

I was captivated by this message but troubled by it at the same time. Right in the middle of the book I stopped and had a conversation with the Lord. "Lord, let's talk this over. I love your mother and she's done a lot in my life, but this insistence on consecration could present a big problem for other people. I'm willing to be consecrated to Mary, but I don't know about anyone else. Now if I were you Lord, I'd do things differently. I question the wisdom of making such a fuss over your mother."

I knew in that moment that I had a choice. I could try to argue with the Lord and figure out his purpose, or I could simply surrender. It's not necessary to understand in order to yield to God. In fact, I think it pleases him when we're willing to receive what he's offering us before we fully understand it. Often it's in the act of surrender that we begin to understand. So it was for me regarding consecration to the Immaculate Heart of Mary. What happened for both Al and me as a result of this deeper consecration is akin to the Baptism of the Holy Spirit. It's not that we now have a greater intellectual knowledge about Mary, but we have a deeper relationship with her through our consecration. And our eyes have been opened to God's amazing plan to use her in the salvation of the world.

Magnificat

In the summer of 1988, twenty years after graduation, I made a visit back to Duquesne. There in the University chapel I knelt before a beautiful wooden statue of Mary. Over her heart she embraced the Holy Spirit and beneath her feet was the word "Magnificat." Tears of gratitude and prayers of thanks overflowed as I considered God's blessings in my life. From my earliest days, through my college years and beyond, grace upon grace has been showered upon me. Deserving nothing, I have received everything. To whatever measure I have remained faithful to God, I owe it all to the prayers of the Blessed Virgin Mary. She has watched over me with her maternal love and protection. Indeed, "Who am I that the mother of my Lord should come to me?"

May this, my own "Magnificat," unite me more deeply to her song of praise and stand as a tribute to her motherly love. With you, dear Mother, I proclaim, "God who is mighty has done great things for me and holy is his name" (Luke 1:49).

NOTES

1. Copyright 1989, Patti Gallagher Mansfield. Published with permission.

Appendix B

EXPERIENCES OF OTHER CHRISTIANS

I am grateful to the persons below who shared with me their experiences of Mary and gave me permission to share them here. I regret not being able to use all the testimonies received.

1. An Indian Boy Converted

In my early years I was a real troublemaker, a serious troublemaker. In the ninth grade I got involved with adults in a strike, climbed into an empty bus, poured petrol on the interior of the bus. Someone else lit the petrol before I had made my preparations to get out. My leg got stuck in one of the seats. I had to tear it to get out. My parents took me to the hospital, where through our Lady's mercy I was healed. In thanksgiving my parents took me on pilgrimage to the shrine of our Lady of Velankanni. As I returned, I found I could hardly talk. Something deep inside me had happened. I began praying the Rosary and found God. My life completely changed. Today I am a candidate for a Marian religious community.

K. S.

2. A Jewish Girl Finds Mary

I was raised in an observant Jewish home. Because of my interest in psychology and religion, after college I began a graduate program at a Christian theological school, still identifying myself as Jewish. In the course of my studies, it became clear to me that Jesus was the Messiah. I thought, "This is what Christians believe, so now I guess I am a Christian. Shouldn't I get baptized?" I had no theological difficulty with openly identifying myself as a Christian or with baptism. The questions I had were more what I would now call "culture shock." Those Christians had different holidays than we, they ate different foods and told different jokes . . . would I be leaving everything I grew up with? Would I betray my grandparents who suffered persecution when they came to the United States, and our distant cousins who remained in Europe and died in the concentration camps?

In the midst of this struggle over whether to be baptized, I went to pray in the chapel of the local Newman Center. There was a statue of Mary in the corner by the altar, a very simple statue in which she looked like the poor young peasant that she was. I heard these words: "I was a Jewish girl too." I knew then that Mary had asked some of the same questions as myself, and that like her I could become a Christian without betraying my people. A few weeks later I was baptized.

S. F.

3. **Mary the Matchmaker**

The year was 1958. I was 27 and still unmarried. I was making the Solemn Novena to our Lady for a special intention: that I would have a date for New Year's Eve. The novena ended on December 8, and when Mom and I returned home, my dad said my friend had called and I was to call her back. I did. To my surprise she wanted to know if I wanted a date for New Year's Eve. I remember telling her that the Blessed Mother really answered my prayer much more quickly than I thought possible. I immediately said "yes" and she was so shocked at my quick response that she wanted to know if I didn't want time to think about it and call her back. I told her it would be a slap in the Blessed Mother's face if I didn't say yes. It was my first date with my future beloved husband, John, to whom I have been happily married 29 years. It was a long wait, but the Blessed Mother saved the best for me, and I am most grateful.

In 1965, after finding out that we could not have biological children, we turned to our Blessed Mother. Seven months later we were approved for adoption. Mary Kay, age 4 weeks, became a member of our family on September 10. She is now 23 years old and the joy of our life. Thank you, Mary! We named her for you!

Today we both belong to a lay Marian community.

J. E.

4. **A Parish Priest and a Parishioner's Problem with Mary**

This evening at our prayer meeting a lady said to me that my homilies on the Blessed Mother confused her and made her feel guilty. Since she came to know the Lord and his love and began to grow in her prayer life, she had not felt the need of Mary or any other of the saints. She was reared in a home where the rosary was recited each night, and if you were falling asleep, you had to kneel out in the open with no support; she believes that those years were wasted in terms of spiritual growth; if she had known the Lord she could have been growing and so she seems to put the rosary and all devotion to Mary in the same bag and feels that my promoting shared prayer, prayer from the heart and also the rosary is contradictory and confusing.

I told her that I was at that point once myself when I did not pray the rosary; I did not feel guilty about it either; I had the Lord. But I do not think I could really love Mary now if I had not come into a deep relationship with the Lord first. I suggested to her that she ask Jesus to reveal his mother to her.

Fr. V. L.

5. Intercession for a Friend

Mary's messages (from Medjugorje) have really simplified and deepened my prayer life. They have also given me a new perspective on the power of selfsacrifice for the good of others. About nine months ago, I began asking Mary to intercede in the life of a very dear friend. She had had no religious life growing up. Her parents never even had her baptized. Feeling a need to begin a serious petition for her, I knelt down one day and promised to pray for her through Mary each day and to give up all sweets. It was only a short time before Christmas, and even though I knew it might be hard, I decided to extend my sacrifice until the day my friend would be baptized. I knew that it was likely I'd be giving up sweets for more than one Christmas!

Very soon after this my friend stopped calling me. Previously we had talked every couple of weeks. Christmas passed and there was no word from her. My calls weren't returned, even though I had left messages. I was feeling saddened, but persisted more than ever in my prayer and sacrifice for her. Finally, midway through Lent, I got her on the phone. We talked for a long time, catching up on the happenings of the previous months. After about forty-five minutes of conversation, she said she had a surprise for me. She said that she was going to be baptized, confirmed and to receive her First Communion the next day! After hanging up the phone, I sat grinning at my kitchen table. I heard a knock at the door. I opened it to find my neighbor standing there with a big plate of cookies. And they were still hot!

M. D.

6. A Feminist Convert Discovers Mary

I converted to Roman Catholicism in 1977 at the age of 24 from a Southern Baptist background. Some parts of my new faith, like the sacrament of reconciliation, I welcomed with open arms. But for eleven years I had a complete psychological block against Mary. I either felt a complete void or mild hostility.

The factors that caused my antiMary stance were: One, my Baptist upbringing, which taught that we should pray only to God. Two, in the faith of my childhood Mary was of no importance. She was usually mentioned only at Christmas. Certainly we had no relationship with her! Last, I grew up to be a vehement feminist, and Mary seemed to be everything a feminist fought against. I read such pamphlets as *Mary, the Masochist* and *Mary the Doormat*. And I believed what I read.

163

But underneath my surface smugness I felt an increasing uneasiness and pain. People I profoundly admired, such as the late Bishop Bernard Topel, loved and reverenced Mary. "Mary is your mother," he stated with heartfelt firmness at the end of one homily, "And she loves you." He signed all his correspondence, "Yours in the service of our Lady." When I spoke slightingly of Mary, as a Jesuit priest was driving me home from a prayer meeting, he stopped the car and astounded me by shouting, "Do you want to walk home?" He shouted angrily, "I don't think it's right to talk like that about someone else's mother!" So many Catholic books and magazines attached great importance to Mary and demonstrated immense respect for her. Songs were sung expressing the deepest tenderness and admiration for her.

Slowly over the years I began to feel I was missing out on someone special. I even prayed some years ago to Jesus, expressing my grief and giving him permission to change my attitude about his mother. Still no break-through. I still felt cold and indifferent when Mary's name was mentioned or prayers to her were said. And I continued to be confused as to how I could be a feminist and love Mary also.

Over the years some warmth began to develop. I began to be touched by the image of Mary and the Infant Jesus as portrayed by statues, necklaces, paintings, etc. I was moved by tender songs sung to her. I began to dislike hearing Mary's name spoken with disrespect. And I was disturbed when the word Madonna was mentioned and more people seemed to think of the singer than of the mother of our Lord.

Then in late 1987 a Marianist priest, Father Florian, invited me to visit him in his community in Bangalore,

India (I had been living and working in Nepal). The word Marianist meant nothing to me. It was just one more religious community. I took Father Florian up on his offer and visited his community in February 1988. From the first day it was obvious that Mary was of central importance in Marianist community life. Prayers to her were offered; songs to her were sung, but what struck me so deeply were the personal testimonies to Mary's intercessory powers, and the radiant faces filled with love and trust in Mary.

I began to throw every objection I had against Mary at the priests and brothers. They weren't the least bit shaken and responded to every taunt with calm conviction. The last day of my visit I was afraid to board the train because, at times in India, bandits attack the trains and the passengers on them. Brother Richard, the superior of the house suggested, "Pray to Mary for protection."

"Do you really believe that?" I asked.

His face transfigured with joy, he exclaimed, "Oh, yes! With Mary's help obstacles just melt away." Then he told me of being on a train on which dacoits robbed all the passengers of their jewelry and valuables.

"Where was your Mary then?" I sneered.

"No one was killed," he replied. "No one was harmed."

That night, desperately afraid, I did pray to Mary for protection. I reached my destination safely. Perhaps I would have anyway, but I remembered to thank Mary.

From that day my psychological impediment against Mary was gone—completely. I felt as though I had fallen in love. I felt I had a new relationship in my life. For several weeks I sensed Mary's loving presence almost continuously. I realized that Mary had always been there waiting for my response. I was able to pray to her easily, and I begged her forgiveness for neglecting her all these years. When I read about Mary I feel tenderness. When someone thanks God for Mary or a hymn to her is sung, my heart says an emphatic, "Yes!" I dedicated my recent eight-day retreat to Mary and asked her to make my faith life mirror hers.

And surprisingly, I no longer feel any contradiction in loving Mary and in being a feminist. The Bible is full of women fulfilling different roles—as judges, generals, prophetesses, deaconesses, queens, etc. Mary did the will of God for her life. God's will for Mary and God's will for each of us is different. We are to be like Mary insofar as we find God's will for our lives and obey it whole-heartedly.

M. B.

7. Mary and a Compulsive Habit

Seven years ago a friend shared with me that ever since she was a child she had chewed her fingernails, keeping them always ragged and much shorter than nails should be. For nearly forty years of her life, though she had tried all the remedies recommended, she been unable to break this nervous, compulsive, humiliating habit. I suggested we ask Mary for a cure not just of the compulsive habit but of whatever root it might be coming from deep within her. We began praying together when we could, and I would ask Mary to respond to my friend as one woman to another. I invited her to stroke her nails to increase her awareness of them and to ask Mary to help her become aware of these sensations whenever she felt the compulsion to chew her nails, so that she could make a conscious effort to stop chewing, be fully aware of all the feelings around that effort, then, with Mary's help, to go on about whatever she had to do.

At the beginning, all seemed futile, but very slowly over several months of prayer, conscious sensation of the nails and the presence and help of Mary, she noted progress. After a year she felt that not only was there less compulsion to chew, but also that the period of continued growth of the nails was stretching out. Friends began to notice a change in her hands and nails. After a few months more, the compulsion of forty years was completely gone, and now she has actually begun to help other compulsive nail-chewers through the same process: prayer, conscious sensation through stroking of the nails, and the presence of Mary.

G. D.

8. Convert and Mother

My husband grew up near St. Anthony School for Exceptional Children and used to sneak over there at night, as a Protestant teenager, to pray in front of a statue of Mary on the grounds. I always prayed "Hail Mary's" when I was scared, even when I went through my late teens and early twenties. There is something really compelling about Mary. Even if I had confused ideas about God and Jesus, I thought it was vastly comforting to think that Mary might pray for me. Early in our marriage, we lived in New Hampshire, and we always went back to Pittsburgh for Christmas, driving through Vermont and New Hampshire on treacherous, icy mountain roads. I would be terrified and, still a Protestant, sit there silently praying one "Hail Mary" after another. We never got in an accident on those trips, although we had some close calls. I was terrified of auto accidents then, because I had recently been in such a bad one, the one that left me with my extensive scar collection.

Now that I am a Catholic I feel I belong to a church that, even without the ordination of women, makes room for the feminine, the gentle, the intuitive and the nurturing aspects of the divine nature. Even if Catholics envisioned a macho God, at least they had Mary to soften him up! (Bad theology, I guess, but that was my feeling.) As a simple woman, Mary is not ethereal. A person whose body bleeds every month and who feels more or less rotten when it does, and whose body can be taken over by a little growing creature who gets the nutrients first and who may, as I experienced with my son, decide to have an exercise hour (the Kick-Mom-so-she-can't-sleep period) from 2 to 3 a.m. can hardly feel ethereal if she tries!

E. C.

9. Danger in the Indian Jungle

We had been giving retreats in North India to some of the poorest Christian villagers. As a Santhal tribal and now a Marianist novice, I was accompanying Sister Usha as a team member, translating for her from Hindi into Santhali and praying and sharing with the villagers. From Hazaribagh we had to go to the village of Saida on foot. After several hours of walking, I was a few minutes ahead of Sister Usha and her companion, a girl from Saida. We had been told that ahead we would have to traverse a two-hour stretch of jungle infamous for its dacoits (robbers). When my companion and I reached the entrance to the jungle, two strangers with bicycles accosted me and began pumping questions at me: "Where are you coming from?" "Hazaribagh," I said. "Where are you going?" "To Saida." "Are you from Saida?" I could tell they were trying to find out if I was a stranger, an easier prey for dacoits. "Yes, I am," I said, hoping this would satisfy them and not reveal that I was a stranger (they had no right to ask anyway). "How big a village is it?" "About 300 families," I guessed in my answer. "How long does it take to get there?" "About two hours on foot," I relayed what I had been told.

As they saw Sr. Usha and the girl coming, they got on their bicycles and took the narrow path into the jungle. The four of us sat down. The girl from Saida said, "Why did you tell them we were going to Saida? These are the gundas (thugs) and they will be waiting for us in the jungle." And that meant they would waylay us, rob us, possibly beat us and tie us up some place off the path (if not actually kill us) and leave us there till someone might rescue us or we could work out our escape. What to do? We decided to sit down and take a short rest first. All kinds of thoughts and fears were going through my mind. I turned to Mother Mary and said, "Mother Mary, whatever is going to happen I accept, but I ask your help to take care of us."

We plunged into the jungle and walked and walked. An hour into our journey there were footsteps behind us. Looking back I saw two men approaching. My God, I thought, this is it.

"*Gisu Moran,* Sister!" they said. I couldn't believe it! That's the Christian Santhali greeting, "Praise Jesus!" They had recognized Sister Usha from the religious sari she was wearing. These were two Christian Santhals from the village to which we were going. They were our

169

guardian angels all the way to Saida—Mother Mary's answer to my prayer.

S. T.

10. A Protestant Theologian, Hippies and the Holy Mother

(The following account appeared in the Protestant review, *Reformed Journal,* 39 [February 1989] 5-6, and is reproduced here with permission.)

Recently I read another evangelical critique of Roman Catholicism's Marian doctrines. I was in basic agreement with the points that were made. I find it difficult to know why Roman Catholics say what they do about the status of Mary.

But I do wish that the tone of the criticisms had been a little gentler. While my theological convictions on this topic are still firm, my mood has gotten a little softer in the last year or so, ever since the afternoon when I found myself breathing a short but heartfelt prayer to the Holy Mother.

It was in a cathedral in northern France, on a lazy summer day in July of 1987. As a way of giving some focus to our vacation wanderings, my wife and I were making a point of visiting Gothic cathedrals.

As we approached this particular cathedral, a young couple on a motorcycle pulled up. They were in their late teens. They were decked out in a style that was very punk: both were dressed in black; his hair was spiked, hers was dyed orange; her face was heavily painted in white and black.

I was curious about why they were visiting a cathedral. So while my wife studied the art, I followed this couple at a discreet distance as they walked around.

Actually, they swaggered. I caught nothing of their conversation, but their insolence was unmistakable. She would point at something derisively, and he would snort. Then he would point and she would snort. Whatever the purpose of their visit, I decided, it had nothing to do with either a spiritual or an aesthetic appreciation for the contents of Gothic cathedrals.

I lingered longer than they did at the high altar, so I don't know how the change of mood occurred. But when I came upon them again, she was standing near a statue of the Virgin Mary in a side chapel, while he was a little ways off, looking at a painting. The young woman was staring directly into the Holy Mother's face. Mary's eyes were directed toward a little kneeling bench at her feet, and her hands were outstretched.

Suddenly the young woman lurched toward the bench and knelt before the Virgin. Face buried in her arms, she began to sob uncontrollably. Her companion turned and saw her. His face registered shock.

I moved on. Many minutes later, I slowly made my way back to the side chapel. The young woman was just standing up from the kneeling bench. She looked into the Virgin's face, then turned to her friend. Her punk makeup was almost all washed away, and her eyes were very red. She held out her hand, and he took it. Slowly, and without a word, they walked away.

I don't really understand what happened to that young woman that afternoon, and I probably never will. But

I'm glad that she knelt before the Virgin. My hunch is that it was very good for her to shed those tears.

I hope so. I think about that young woman often. And when I remember her, I pray to God on her behalf.

On that afternoon, though, I prayed to the Holy Mother. After the couple left, I sat in a pew in the side chapter, and looked into the face of the statue. "Mary," I asked, "please don't let her wander far. Keep her safe, and lead her to your Son."

That is the only time I have ever addressed a petition to the Virgin Mary. I don't know whether that one prayer makes me guilty of "Mariolatry" or not. Nor has the question troubled me much.

The theology that I instinctively operated with on that summer afternoon may have been confused. But I still sense that my prayer arrived at the right destination. Which means that my tone will be a little softer from here on when I debate the Marian doctrines with my Catholic friends.

Richard J. Mouw

11. From a Jailed Rescuer

[The following excerpts are from two letters received from a young man held in jail for blocking entry to an abortion clinic. Before his incarceration he was preparing himself to make St. Louis de Montfort's Consecration to Mary. Unable to do it in the context of the liturgy, he completed it in jail.]

If one were going to embark on a journey intended to have its endpoint in perfection of the soul, where would he start? I have finished the Consecration and found it to be an immense help. My sense of abandonment and a kind of indifference to my situation have deepened markedly. Even just today I noticed, to my great amusement, that I had a keen sense of joy just walking around during "yard." I was where I was supposed to be, and doing what I was supposed to do, and God was pleased. It seemed funny that I could meet God walking around in circles, but it seemed so. So I did it as well as I could. But God showed me the peace of being in his plan and I didn't want anything else. Just walking around in circles... I would like to continue not only being in God's will today but growing so I can be in it tomorrow— beyond walking around in circles! I feel like I'm very new to all this. I have made very sincere pleas to God in the past, asking Him to sanctify and perfect me, but they were kind of like a clear "rational moment" and the prayer was uttered with true desire and fervor but then I got busy with the "real world" again. Now, however, I seem to have a more conscious continuous longing to begin moving towards sanctity and a true interior life.

Consecration to Mary. You simply can't imagine the vast amount of grace that has been poured out on me in this devotion. I wish the whole world could be made to understand how quickly Mary takes us to Christ. A single smile from God's own Mother is enough to bless generations of men! It was funny that you happened to think you might need my prayers more than I needed yours. I try to tell people all the time that I've been given the best thing around by being in here [jail]. You would all stop writing to me and feeling sorry for me if you had even an inkling as to how much Mary blesses those who sacrifice for her Son! There is simply nothing better on this earth, no better way to know the deepest mysteries

173

of Christ's heart, than to suffer for Him and with Him. The only pity is it's such a well kept secret. I continue to pray that somehow everyone will come to understand this.